A Treatise on Parents and Children

George Bernard Shaw

A Treatise on Parents and Children

George Bernard Shaw

PO Box 2211
Fairfield, IA 52556
www.1stworldlibrary.org
First Edition

LCCN: 2003099906

ISBN: 1-59540-235-7

Purchase *"A Treatise on Parents and Children"*
as a traditional bound book at:
www.1stWorldLibrary.org/purchase.asp?ISBN=1-59540-235-7

A Treatise on Parents And Children

contributed by the Charles Family

in support of

1st World Library Literary Society

CONTENTS

PARENTS AND CHILDREN

Trailing Clouds of Glory

Childhood is a stage in the process of that continual remanufacture of the Life Stuff by which the human race is perpetuated. The Life Force either will not or cannot achieve immortality except in very low organisms: indeed it is by no means ascertained that even the amoeba is immortal. Human beings visibly wear out, though they last longer than their friends the dogs. Turtles, parrots, and elephants are believed to be capable of outliving the memory of the oldest human inhabitant. But the fact that new ones are born conclusively proves that they are not immortal. Do away with death and you do away with the need for birth: in fact if you went on breeding, you would finally have to kill old people to make room for young ones.

Now death is not necessarily a failure of energy on the part of the Life Force. People with no imagination try to make things which will last for ever, and even want to live for ever themselves. But the intelligently imaginative man knows very well that it is waste of labor to make a machine that will last ten years, because it will probably be superseded in half that time by an improved machine answering the same purpose.

He also knows that if some devil were to convince us that our dream of personal immortality is no dream but a hard fact, such a shriek of despair would go up from the human race as no other conceivable horror could provoke. With all our perverse nonsense as to John Smith living for a thousand million eons and for ever after, we die voluntarily, knowing that it is time for us to be scrapped, to be remanufactured, to come back, as Wordsworth divined, trailing ever brightening clouds of glory. We must all be born again, and yet again and again. We should like to live a little longer just as we should like 50 pounds: that is, we should take it if we could get it for nothing; but that sort of idle liking is not will. It is amazing - considering the way we talk - how little a man will do to get 50 pounds: all the 50-pound notes I have ever known of have been more easily earned than a laborious sixpence; but the difficulty of inducing a man to make any serious effort to obtain 50 pounds is nothing to the difficulty of inducing him to make a serious effort to keep alive. The moment he sees death approach, he gets into bed and sends for a doctor. He knows very well at the back of his conscience that he is rather a poor job and had better be remanufactured. He knows that his death will make room for a birth; and he hopes that it will be a birth of something that he aspired to be and fell short of. He knows that it is through death and rebirth that this corruptible shall become incorruptible, and this mortal put on immortality. Practise as you will on his ignorance, his fears, and his imagination, with bribes of paradises and threats of hells, there is only one belief that can rob death of its sting and the grave of its victory; and that is the belief that we can lay down the burden of our wretched little makeshift individualities for ever at each lift towards the goal of evolution, which can only be a being that cannot be improved upon. After all, what man is capable of the insane self-conceit of believing that an eternity of himself would be tolerable even to himself? Those who try to believe it postulate that they shall be made perfect first. But if you make me perfect I shall no longer be myself, nor will it be possible for me to conceive my present imperfections (and what I cannot conceive I cannot remember); so that you may just as well give me a new name and face the fact that I am a new person and that the old Bernard Shaw is as dead as mutton. Thus, oddly enough, the conventional belief in the matter comes to this: that if you wish to live for ever you must be wicked enough to be irretrievably damned, since the saved are no longer what they were, and in hell alone do people retain their sinful nature: that is to say, their individuality. And this sort of hell, however convenient as a means of intimidating persons who have practically no honor and no conscience, is not a fact. Death is for many of us the gate of hell; but we are inside on the way out, not outside on the way in. Therefore let us give up telling one another idle stories, and rejoice in death as we rejoice in birth; for without death we cannot be born again; and the man who does not wish to be born again and born better is fit only to represent the City of London in Parliament, or perhaps the university of Oxford.

The Child is Father to the Man

Is he? Then in the name of common sense why do we always treat children on the assumption that the man is father to the child? Oh, these fathers! And we are not content with fathers: we must have godfathers, forgetting that the child is godfather to the man. Has it ever struck you as curious that in a country where the first article of belief is that every child is born with a godfather whom we all call "our father which art in heaven," two very limited individual mortals should be allowed to appear at its baptism and explain that they are its godparents, and that they will look after its salvation until it is no longer a child. I had a godmother who made herself responsible in this way for me. She presented me with a Bible with a gilt clasp and edges, larger than the Bibles similarly presented to my sisters, because my sex entitled me to a heavier article. I must have seen that lady at least four times in the twenty years following. She never alluded to my salvation in any way. People occasionally ask me to act as godfather to their children with a levity which convinces me that they have not the faintest notion that it involves anything more than calling the helpless child George Bernard without regard to the possibility that it may grow up in the liveliest abhorrence of my notions.

A person with a turn for logic might argue that if God

is the Father of all men, and if the child is father to the man, it follows that the true representative of God at the christening is the child itself. But such posers are unpopular, because they imply that our little customs, or, as we often call them, our religion, mean something, or must originally have meant something, and that we understand and believe that something.

However, my business is not to make confusion worse confounded, but to clear it up. Only, it is as well to begin by a sample of current thought and practice which shews that on the subject of children we are very deeply confused. On the whole, whatever our theory or no theory may be, our practice is to treat the child as the property of its immediate physical parents, and to allow them to do what they like with it as far as it will let them. It has no rights and no liberties: in short, its condition is that which adults recognize as the most miserable and dangerous politically possible for themselves: namely, the condition of slavery. For its alleviation we trust to the natural affection of the parties, and to public opinion. A father cannot for his own credit let his son go in rags. Also, in a very large section of the population, parents finally become dependent on their children. Thus there are checks on child slavery which do not exist, or are less powerful, in the case of manual and industrial slavery. Sensationally bad cases fall into two classes, which are really the same class: namely, the children whose parents are excessively addicted to the sensual luxury of petting children, and the children whose parents are excessively addicted to the sensual luxury of physically torturing them. There is a Society for the Prevention of Cruelty to Children which has effectually made an end of our belief that mothers are any more to be trusted than stepmothers, or fathers than slave-drivers. And there is a growing body of law designed to prevent parents from using their children ruthlessly to make money for the household. Such legislation has always been furiously resisted by the parents, even when the horrors of factory slavery were at their worst; and the extension of such legislation at present would be impossible if it were not that the parents affected by it cannot control a majority of votes in Parliament. In domestic life a great deal of service is done by children, the girls acting as nursemaids and general servants, and the lads as errand boys. In the country both boys and girls do a substantial share of farm labor. This is why it is necessary to coerce poor parents to send their children to school, though in the relatively small class which keeps plenty of servants it is impossible to induce parents to keep their children at home instead of paying schoolmasters to take them off their hands.

It appears then that the bond of affection between parents and children does not save children from the slavery that denial of rights involves in adult political relations. It sometimes intensifies it, sometimes mitigates it; but on the whole children and parents confront one another as two classes in which all the political power is on one side; and the results are not at all unlike what they would be if there were no immediate consanguinity between them, and one were white and the other black, or one enfranchised and the other disenfranchised, or one ranked as gentle and the other simple. Not that Nature counts for nothing in the case and political rights for everything. But a denial of political rights, and the resultant delivery of one class into the mastery of another, affects their relations so extensively and profoundly that it is impossible to ascertain what the real natural relations of the two classes are until this political relation is abolished.

What is a Child?

An experiment. A fresh attempt to produce the just man made perfect: that is, to make humanity divine. And you will vitiate the experiment if you make the slightest attempt to abort it into some fancy figure of your own: for example, your notion of a good man or a womanly woman. If you treat it as a little wild beast to be tamed, or as a pet to be played with, or even as a means to save you trouble and to make money for you (and these are our commonest ways), it may fight its way through in spite of you and save its soul alive; for all its instincts will resist you, and possibly be strengthened in the resistance; but if you begin with its own holiest aspirations, and suborn them for your own purposes, then there is hardly any limit to the mischief you may do. Swear at a child, throw your boots at it, send it flying from the room with a cuff or a kick; and the experience will be as instructive to the child as a difficulty with a short-tempered dog or a bull. Francis Place tells us that his father always struck his children when he found one within his reach. The effect on the young Places seems to have been simply to make them keep out of their father's way, which was no doubt what he desired, as far as he desired anything at all. Francis records the habit without bitterness, having reason to thank his stars that his father respected the inside of his head whilst cuffing the outside of it; and this made it easy for Francis to do yeoman's service to his country as that rare and admirable thing, a Freethinker: the only sort of thinker, I may remark, whose thoughts, and consequently whose religious convictions, command any respect.

Now Mr Place, senior, would be described by many as a bad father; and I do not contend that he was a conspicuously good one. But as compared with the conventional good father who deliberately imposes himself on his son as a god; who takes advantage of childish credulity and parent worship to persuade his son that what he approves of is right and what he disapproves of is wrong; who imposes a corresponding conduct on the child by a system of prohibitions and penalties, rewards and eulogies, for which he claims divine sanction: compared to this sort of abortionist and monster maker, I say, Place appears almost as a Providence. Not that it is possible to live with children any more than with grown-up people without imposing rules of conduct on them. There is a point at which every person with human nerves has to say to a child "Stop that noise." But suppose the child asks why! There are various answers in use. The simplest: "Because it irritates me," may fail; for it may strike the child as being rather amusing to irritate you; also the child, having comparatively no nerves, may be unable to conceive your meaning vividly enough. In any case it may want to make a noise more than to spare your feelings. You may therefore have to explain that the effect of the irritation will be that you will do something unpleasant if the noise continues. The something unpleasant may be only a look of suffering to rouse the child's affectionate sympathy (if it has any), or it may run to forcible expulsion from the room with plenty of unnecessary violence; but the principle is the same: there are no false pretences involved: the child learns in a straightforward way that it does not pay to be inconsiderate. Also, perhaps, that Mamma, who made the child learn the Sermon on the Mount, is not really a Christian.

The Sin of Nadab and Abihu

But there is another sort of answer in wide use which is neither straightforward, instructive, nor harmless. In its simplest form it substitutes for "Stop that noise," "Dont be naughty," which means that the child, instead of annoying you by a perfectly healthy and natural infantile procedure, is offending God. This is a blasphemous lie; and the fact that it is on the lips of every nurserymaid does not excuse it in the least. Dickens tells us of a nurserymaid who elaborated it into "If you do that, angels wont never love you." I remember a servant who used to tell me that if I were not good, by which she meant if I did not behave with a single eye to her personal convenience, the cock would come down the chimney. Less imaginative but equally dishonest people told me I should go to hell if I did not make myself agreeable to them. Bodily violence, provided it be the hasty expression of normal provoked resentment and not vicious cruelty, cannot harm a child as this sort of pious fraud harms it. There is a legal limit to physical cruelty; and there are also human limits to it. There is an active Society which brings to book a good many parents who starve and torture and overwork their children, and intimidates a good many more. When parents of this type are caught, they are treated as criminals; and not infrequently the police have some trouble to save them from being lynched. The people against whom children are wholly unprotected are those who devote themselves to the very mischievous and cruel sort of abortion which is called bringing up a child in the way it should go. Now nobody knows the way a child should go. All the ways discovered so far lead to the horrors of our existing civilizations, described quite justifiably by Ruskin as heaps of agonizing human maggots, struggling with one another for scraps of food. Pious fraud is an attempt to pervert that precious and sacred thing the child's conscience into an instrument of our own convenience, and to use that wonderful and terrible power called Shame to grind our own axe. It is the sin of stealing fire from the altar: a sin so impudently practised by popes, parents, and pedagogues, that one can hardly expect the nurserymaids to see any harm in stealing a few cinders when they are worrited.

Into the blackest depths of this violation of children's souls one can hardly bear to look; for here we find pious fraud masking the violation of the body by obscene cruelty. Any parent or school teacher who takes a secret and abominable delight in torture is allowed to lay traps into which every child must fall, and then beat it to his or her heart's content. A gentleman once wrote to me and said, with an obvious conviction that he was being most reasonable and high minded, that the only thing he beat his children for was failure in perfect obedience and perfect truthfulness. On these attributes, he said, he must insist. As one of them is not a virtue at all, and the other is the attribute of a god, one can imagine what the lives of this gentleman's children would have been if it had been possible for him to live down to his monstrous and foolish pretensions. And yet he might have written his letter to The Times (he very nearly did, by the way) without incurring any danger of being removed to an asylum, or even losing his reputation for taking a very proper view of his parental duties. And at least it was not a trivial view, nor an ill meant one. It was much more respectable than the general consensus of opinion that if a school teacher can devise a question a child cannot answer, or overhear it calling omega omeega, he or she may beat the child viciously. Only, the cruelty must be whitewashed by a moral excuse, and a pretence of reluctance. It must be for the child's good. The assailant must say "This hurts me more than it hurts you." There must be hypocrisy as well as cruelty. The injury to the child would be far less if the voluptuary said frankly "I beat you because I like beating you; and I shall do it whenever I can contrive an excuse for it." But to represent this detestable lust to the child as Divine wrath, and the cruelty as the beneficent act of God, which is exactly what all our floggers do, is to add to the torture of the body, out of which the flogger at least gets some pleasure, the maiming and blinding of the child's soul, which can bring nothing but horror to anyone.

The Manufacture of Monsters

This industry is by no means peculiar to China. The Chinese (they say) make physical monsters. We revile them for it and proceed to make moral monsters of our own children. The most excusable parents are those who try to correct their own faults in their offspring. The parent who says to his child: "I am one of the successes of the Almighty: therefore imitate me in every particular or I will have the skin off your back" (a quite common attitude) is a much more absurd figure than the man who, with a pipe in his mouth, thrashes his boy for smoking. If you must hold yourself up to your children as an object lesson (which is not at all necessary), hold yourself up as a warning and not as an example. But you had much better let the child's character alone. If you once allow yourself to regard a child as so much material for you to manufacture into any shape that happens to suit your fancy you are defeating the experiment of the Life Force. You are assuming that the child does not know its own business, and that you do. In this you are sure to be wrong: the child feels the drive of the Life Force (often called the Will of God); and you cannot feel it for him. Handel's parents no doubt thought they knew better than their child when they tried to prevent his becoming a musician. They would have been equally wrong and equally unsuccessful if they had tried to prevent the child becoming a great rascal had its genius lain in that direction. Handel would have been Handel, and Napoleon and Peter of Russia themselves in spite of all the parents in creation, because, as often happens, they were stronger than their parents. But this does not happen always. Most children can be, and many are, hopelessly warped and wasted by parents who are ignorant and silly enough to suppose that they know what a human being ought to be, and who stick at nothing in their determination to force their children into their moulds. Every child has a right to its own bent. It has a right to be a Plymouth Brother though its parents be convinced atheists. It has a right to dislike its mother or father or sister or brother or uncle or aunt if they are antipathetic to it. It has a right to find its own way and go its own way, whether that way seems wise or foolish to others, exactly as an adult has. It has a right to privacy as to its own doings and its own affairs as much as if it were its own father.

Small and Large Families

These rights have now become more important than they used to be, because the modern practice of limiting families enables them to be more effectually violated. In a family of ten, eight, six, or even four children, the rights of the younger ones to a great extent take care of themselves and of the rights of the elder ones too. Two adult parents, in spite of a house to keep and an income to earn, can still interfere to a disastrous extent with the rights and liberties of one child. But by the time a fourth child has arrived, they are not only outnumbered two to one, but are getting tired of the thankless and mischievous job of bringing up their children in the way they think they should go. The old observation that members of large families get on in the world holds good because in large families it is impossible for each child to receive what schoolmasters call "individual attention." The children may receive a good deal of individual attention from one another in the shape of outspoken reproach, ruthless ridicule, and violent resistance to their attempts at aggression; but the parental despots are compelled by the multitude of their subjects to resort to political rather than personal rule, and to spread their attempts at moral monster-making over so many children, that each child has enough freedom, and enough sport in the prophylactic process of laughing at its elders behind their backs, to escape with much less damage than the single child. In a large school the system may be bad; but the personal influence of the head master has to be exerted, when it is exerted at all, in a public way, because he has little more power of working on the affections of the individual scholar in the intimate way that, for example, the mother of a single child can, than the prime minister has of working on the affections of any individual voter.

Children as Nuisances

Experienced parents, when children's rights are preached to them, very naturally ask whether children are to be allowed to do what they like. The best reply is to ask whether adults are to be allowed to do what they like. The two cases are the same. The adult who is nasty is not allowed to do what he likes: neither can the child who likes to be nasty. There is no difference in principle between the rights of a child and those of an adult: the difference in their cases is one of circumstance. An adult is not supposed to be punished except by process of law; nor, when he is so punished, is the person whom he has injured allowed to act as judge, jury, and executioner. It is true that employers do act in this way every day to their workpeople; but this is not a justified and intended part of the situation: it is an abuse of Capitalism which nobody defends in principle. As between child and parent or nurse it is not argued about because it is inevitable. You cannot hold an impartial judicial inquiry every time a child misbehaves itself. To allow the child to misbehave without instantly making it unpleasantly conscious of the fact would be to spoil it. The adult has therefore to take action of some sort with nothing but his conscience to shield the child from injustice or unkindness. The action may be a torrent of scolding culminating in a furious smack causing terror and pain, or it may be a remonstrance causing remorse, or it may be a sarcasm causing shame and humiliation, or it may be a sermon causing the child to believe that it is a little reprobate on the road to hell. The child has no defence in any case except the kindness and conscience of the adult; and the adult had better not forget this; for it involves a heavy responsibility.

And now comes our difficulty. The responsibility, being so heavy, cannot be discharged by persons of feeble character or intelligence. And yet people of high character and intelligence cannot be plagued with the care of children. A child is a restless, noisy little animal, with an insatiable appetite for knowledge, and consequently a maddening persistence in asking questions. If the child is to remain in the room with a highly intelligent and sensitive adult, it must be told, and if necessary forced, to sit still and not speak, which is injurious to its health, unnatural, unjust, and therefore cruel and selfish beyond toleration. Consequently the highly intelligent and sensitive adult hands the child over to a nurserymaid who has no nerves and can therefore stand more noise, but who has also no scruples, and may therefore be very bad ompany for the child.

Here we have come to the central fact of the question: a fact nobody avows, which is yet the true explanation of the monstrous system of child imprisonment and torture which we disguise under such hypocrisies as education, training, formation of character and the rest of it. This fact is simply that a child is a nuisance to a grown-up person. What is more, the nuisance becomes more and more intolerable as the grown-up person becomes more cultivated, more sensitive, and more deeply engaged in the highest methods of adult work. The child at play is noisy and ought to be noisy: Sir

Isaac Newton at work is quiet and ought to be quiet. And the child should spend most of its time at play, whilst the adult should spend most of his time at work. I am not now writing on behalf of persons who coddle themselves into a ridiculous condition of nervous feebleness, and at last imagine themselves unable to work under conditions of bustle which to healthy people are cheerful and stimulating. I am sure that if people had to choose between living where the noise of children never stopped and where it was never heard, all the goodnatured and sound people would prefer the incessant noise to the incessant silence. But that choice is not thrust upon us by the nature of things. There is no reason why children and adults should not see just as much of one another as is good for them, no more and no less. Even at present you are not compelled to choose between sending your child to a boarding school (which means getting rid of it altogether on more or less hypocritical pretences) and keeping it continually at home. Most working folk today either send their children to day schools or turn them out of doors. This solves the problem for the parents. It does not solve it for the children, any more than the tethering of a goat in a field or the chasing of an unlicensed dog into the streets solves it for the goat or the dog; but it shews that in no class are people willing to endure the society of their children, and consequently that it is an error to believe that the family provides children with edifying adult society, or that the family is a social unit. The family is in that, as in so many other respects, a humbug. Old people and young people cannot walk at the same pace without distress and final loss of health to one of the parties. When they are sitting indoors they cannot endure the same degrees of temperature and the same supplies of fresh air. Even if the main factors of noise, restlessness, and inquisitiveness are left out of account, children can stand with indifference sights, sounds, smells, and disorders that would make an adult of fifty utterly miserable; whilst on the other hand such adults find a tranquil happiness in conditions which to children mean unspeakable boredom. And since our system is nevertheless to pack them all into the same house and pretend that they are happy, and that this particular sort of happiness is the foundation of virtue, it is found that in discussing family life we never speak of actual adults or actual children, or of realities of any sort, but always of ideals such as The Home, a Mother's Influence, a Father's Care, Filial Piety, Duty, Affection, Family Life, etc. etc., which are no doubt very comforting phrases, but which beg the question of what a home and a mother's influence and a father's care and so forth really come to in practice. How many hours a week of the time when his children are out of bed does the ordinary bread-winning father spend in the company of his children or even in the same building with them? The home may be a thieves' kitchen, the mother a procuress, the father a violent drunkard; or the mother and father may be fashionable people who see their children three or four times a year during the holidays, and then not oftener than they can help, living meanwhile in daily and intimate contact with their valets and lady's-maids, whose influence and care are often dominant in the household. Affection, as distinguished from simple kindliness, may or may not exist: when it does it either depends on qualities in the parties that would produce it equally if they were of no kin to one another, or it is a more or less morbid survival of the nursing passion; for affection between adults (if they are really adult in mind and not merely grown-up children) and creatures so relatively selfish and cruel as children necessarily are without knowing it or meaning it, cannot be called natural: in fact the evidence shews that it is easier to love the company of a dog than of a commonplace child between the ages of six and the beginnings of controlled maturity; for women who cannot bear to be separated from their pet dogs send their children to boarding schools cheerfully. They may say and even believe that in allowing their children to leave home they are sacrificing themselves for their children's good; but there are very few pet dogs who would not be the better for a month or two spent elsewhere than in a lady's lap or roasting on a drawingroom hearthrug. Besides, to allege that children are better continually away from home is to give up the whole popular sentimental theory of the family; yet the dogs are kept and the children are banished.

Child Fanciers

There is, however, a good deal of spurious family affection. There is the clannishness that will make a dozen brothers and sisters who quarrel furiously among themselves close up their ranks and make common cause against a brother-in-law or a sister-in-law. And there is a strong sense of property in children, which often makes mothers and fathers bitterly jealous of allowing anyone else to interfere with their children, whom they may none the less treat very badly. And there is an extremely dangerous craze for children which leads certain people to establish orphanages and baby farms and schools, seizing any pretext for filling their houses with children exactly as some eccentric old ladies and gentlemen fill theirs with cats. In such places the children are the victims of all the caprices of doting affection and all the excesses of lascivious cruelty. Yet the people who have this morbid craze seldom have any difficulty in finding victims. Parents and guardians are so worried by children and so anxious to get rid of them that anyone who is willing to take them off their hands is welcomed and whitewashed. The very people who read with indignation of Squeers and Creakle in the novels of Dickens are quite ready to hand over their own children to Squeers and Creakle, and to pretend that Squeers and Creakle are monsters of the past. But read the autobiography of Stanley the traveller, or sit in the company of men talking about their school-days, and you will soon find that fiction, which must, if it is to be sold and read, stop short of being positively sickening, dare not tell the whole truth about the people to whom children are handed over on educational pretexts. Not very long ago a schoolmaster in Ireland was murdered by his boys; and for reasons which were never made public it was at first decided not to prosecute the murderers. Yet all these flogging schoolmasters and orphanage fiends and baby farmers are "lovers of children." They are really child fanciers (like bird fanciers or dog fanciers) by irresistible natural predilection, never happy unless they are surrounded by their victims, and always certain to make their living by accepting the custody of children, no matter how many alternative occupations may be available. And bear in mind that they are only the extreme instances of what is commonly called natural affection, apparently because it is obviously unnatural.

The really natural feeling of adults for children in the long prosaic intervals between the moments of affectionate impulse is just that feeling that leads them to avoid their care and constant company as a burden beyond bearing, and to pretend that the places they send them to are well conducted, beneficial, and indispensable to the success of the children in after life. The true cry of the kind mother after her little rosary of kisses is "Run away, darling." It is nicer than "Hold your noise, you young devil; or it will be the worse for you"; but fundamentally it means the same thing: that if you compel an adult and a child to live in one another's company either the adult or the child will be miserable. There is nothing whatever unnatural or wrong or shocking in this fact; and there is no harm in it if only it be sensibly faced and provided for. The mischief that it does at present is produced by our efforts to ignore it, or to smother it under a heap of sentimental lies and false pretences.

Childhood as a State of Sin

Unfortunately all this nonsense tends to accumulate as we become more sympathetic. In many families it is still the custom to treat childhood frankly as a state of sin, and impudently proclaim the monstrous principle that little children should be seen and not heard, and to enforce a set of prison rules designed solely to make cohabitation with children as convenient as possible for adults without the smallest regard for the interests, either remote or immediate, of the children. This system tends to produce a tough, rather brutal, stupid, unscrupulous class, with a fixed idea that all enjoyment consists in undetected sinning; and in certain phases of civilization people of this kind are apt to get the upper hand of more amiable and conscientious races and classes. They have the ferocity of a chained dog, and are proud of it. But the end of it is that they are always in chains, even at the height of their military or political success: they win everything on condition that they are afraid to enjoy it. Their civilizations rest on intimidation, which is so necessary to them that when they cannot find anybody brave enough to intimidate them they intimidate themselves and live in a continual moral and political panic. In the end they get found out and bullied. But that is not the point that concerns us here, which is, that they are in some respects better brought up than the children of sentimental people who are always anxious and miserable about their duty to their children, and who end by neither making their children happy nor having a tolerable life for themselves. A selfish tyrant you know where to have, and he (or she) at least does not confuse your affections; but a conscientious and kindly meddler may literally worry you out of your senses. It is fortunate that only very few parents are capable of doing what they conceive their duty continuously or even at all, and that still fewer are tough enough to ride roughshod over their children at home.

School

But please observe the limitation "at home." What private amateur parental enterprise cannot do may be done very effectively by organized professional enterprise in large institutions established for the purpose. And it is to such professional enterprise that parents hand over their children when they can afford it. They send their children to school; and there is, on the whole, nothing on earth intended for innocent people so horrible as a school. To begin with, it is a prison. But it is in some respects more cruel than a prison. In a prison, for instance, you are not forced to read books written by the warders and the governor (who of course would not be warders and governors if they could write readable books), and beaten or otherwise tormented if you cannot remember their utterly unmemorable contents. In the prison you are not forced to sit listening to turnkeys discoursing without charm or interest on subjects that they don't understand and dont care about, and are therefore incapable of making you understand or care about. In a prison they may torture your body; but they do not torture your brains; and they protect you against violence and outrage from your fellow prisoners. In a school you have none of these advantages. With the world's bookshelves loaded with fascinating and inspired books, the very manna sent down from Heaven to feed your souls, you are forced to read a hideous imposture called a school book, written by a man who cannot write: a book from which no human being can learn anything: a book which, though you may decipher it, you cannot in any fruitful sense read, though the enforced attempt will make you loathe the sight of a book all the rest of your life. With millions of acres of woods and valleys and hills and wind and air and birds and streams and fishes and all sorts of instructive and healthy things easily accessible, or with streets and shop windows and crowds and vehicles and all sorts of city delights at the door, you are forced to sit, not in a room with some human grace and comfort or furniture and decoration, but in a stalled pound with a lot of other children, beaten if you talk, beaten if you move, beaten if you cannot prove by answering idiotic questions that even when you escaped from the pound and from the eye of your gaoler, you were still agonizing over his detestable sham books instead of daring to live. And your childish hatred of your gaoler and flogger is nothing to his adult hatred of you; for he is a slave forced to endure your society for his daily bread. You have not even the satisfaction of knowing how you are torturing him and how he loathes you; and you give yourself unnecessary pains to annoy him with furtive tricks and spiteful doing of forbidden things. No wonder he is sometimes provoked to fiendish outbursts of wrath. No wonder men of downright sense, like Dr Johnson, admit that under such circumstances children will not learn anything unless they are so cruelly beaten that they make desperate efforts to memorize words and phrases to escape flagellation. It is a ghastly business, quite beyond words, this schooling.

And now I hear cries of protest arising all round. First my own schoolmasters, or their ghosts, asking whether

I was cruelly beaten at school? No; but then I did not learn anything at school. Dr Johnson's schoolmaster presumably did care enough whether Sam learned anything to beat him savagely enough to force him to lame his mind - for Johnson's great mind was lamed - by learning his lessons. None of my schoolmasters really cared a rap (or perhaps it would be fairer to them to say that their employers did not care a rap and therefore did not give them the necessary caning powers) whether I learnt my lessons or not, provided my father paid my schooling bill, the collection of which was the real object of the school. Consequently I did not learn my school lessons, having much more important ones in hand, with the result that I have not wasted my life trifling with literary fools in taverns as Johnson did when he should have been shaking England with the thunder of his spirit. My schooling did me a great deal of harm and no good whatever: it was simply dragging a child's soul through the dirt; but I escaped Squeers and Creakle just as I escaped Johnson and Carlyle. And this is what happens to most of us. We are not effectively coerced to learn: we stave off punishment as far as we can by lying and trickery and guessing and using our wits; and when this does not suffice we scribble impositions, or suffer extra imprisonments - "keeping in" was the phrase in my time - or let a master strike us with a cane and fall back on our pride at being able to hear it physically (he not being allowed to hit us too hard) to outface the dishonor we should have been taught to die rather than endure. And so idleness and worthlessness on the one hand and a pretence of coercion on the other became a despicable routine. If my schoolmasters had been really engaged in educating me instead of painfully earning their bread by keeping me from annoying my elders they would have turned me out of the school, telling me that I was thoroughly disloyal to it; that I had no intention of learning; that I was mocking and distracting the boys who did wish to learn; that I was a liar and a shirker and a seditious little nuisance; and that nothing could injure me in character and degrade their occupation more than allowing me (much less forcing me) to remain in the school under such conditions. But in order to get expelled, it was necessary commit a crime of such atrocity that the parents of other boys would have threatened to remove their sons sooner than allow them to be schoolfellows with the delinquent. I can remember only one case in which such a penalty was threatened; and in that case the culprit, a boarder, had kissed a housemaid, or possibly, being a handsome youth, been kissed by her. She did not kiss me; and nobody ever dreamt of expelling me. The truth was, a boy meant just so much a year to the institution. That was why he was kept there against his will. That was why he was kept there when his expulsion would have been an unspeakable relief and benefit both to his teachers and himself.

It may be argued that if the uncommercial attitude had been taken, and all the disloyal wasters and idlers shewn sternly to the door, the school would not have been emptied, but filled. But so honest an attitude was impossible. The masters must have hated the school much more than the boys did. Just as you cannot imprison a man without imprisoning a warder to see that he does not escape, the warder being tied to the prison as effectually by the fear of unemployment and starvation as the prisoner is by the bolts and bars, so these poor schoolmasters, with their small salaries and large classes, were as much prisoners as we were, and much more responsible and anxious ones. They could not impose the heroic attitude on their employers; nor would they have been able to obtain places as schoolmasters if their habits had been heroic. For the best of them their employment was provisional: they looked forward to escaping from it into the pulpit. The ablest and most impatient of them were often so irritated by the awkward, slow-witted, slovenly boys: that is, the ones that required special consideration and patient treatment, that they vented their irritation on them ruthlessly, nothing being easier than to entrap or bewilder such a boy into giving a pretext for punishing him.

My Scholastic Acquirements

The results, as far as I was concerned, were what might have been expected. My school made only the thinnest pretence of teaching anything but Latin and Greek. When I went there as a very small boy I knew a good deal of Latin grammar which I had been taught in a few weeks privately by my uncle. When I had been several years at school this same uncle examined me and discovered that the net result of my schooling was that I had forgotten what he had taught me, and had learnt nothing else. To this day, though I can still decline a Latin noun and repeat some of the old paradigms in the old meaningless way, because their rhythm sticks to me, I have never yet seen a Latin inscription on a tomb that I could translate throughout. Of Greek I can decipher perhaps the greater part of the Greek alphabet. In short, I am, as to classical education, another Shakespear. I can read French as easily as English; and under pressure of necessity I can turn to account some scraps of German and a little operatic Italian; but these I was never taught at school. Instead, I was taught lying, dishonorable submission to tyranny, dirty stories, a blasphemous habit of treating love and maternity as obscene jokes, hopelessness, evasion, derision, cowardice, and all the blackguard's shifts by which the coward intimidates other cowards. And if I had been a boarder at an English public school instead of a day boy at an Irish one, I might have had to add to these, deeper shames still.

Schoolmasters of Genius

And now, if I have reduced the ghosts of my schoolmasters to melancholy acquiescence in all this (which everybody who has been at an ordinary school will recognize as true), I have still to meet the much more sincere protests of the handful of people who have a natural genius for "bringing up" children. I shall be asked with kindly scorn whether I have heard of Froebel and Pestalozzi, whether I know the work that is being done by Miss Mason and the Dottoressa Montessori or, best of all as I think, the Eurythmics School of Jacques Dalcroze at Hellerau near Dresden. Jacques Dalcroze, like Plato, believes in saturating his pupils with music. They walk to music, play to music, work to music, obey drill commands that would bewilder a guardsman to music, think to music, live to music, get so clearheaded about music that they can move their several limbs each in a different metre until they become complicated living magazines of cross rhythms, and, what is more, make music for others to do all these things to. Stranger still, though Jacques Dalcroze, like all these great teachers, is the completest of tyrants, knowing what is right and that he must and will have the lesson just so or else break his heart (not somebody else's, observe), yet his school is so fascinating that every woman who sees it exclaims "Oh, why was I not taught like this!" and elderly gentlemen excitedly enrol themselves as students and distract classes of infants by their desperate endeavors to beat two in a bar with one hand and three with the other, and start off on earnest walks round the room, taking two steps backward whenever Monsieur Daleroze calls out "Hop!" Oh yes: I know all about these wonderful schools that you cannot keep children or even adults out of, and these teachers whom their pupils not only obey without coercion, but adore. And if you will tell me roughly how many Masons and Montessoris and Dalcrozes you think you can pick up in Europe for salaries of from thirty shillings to five pounds a week, I will estimate your chances of converting your millions of little scholastic hells into little scholastic heavens. If you are a distressed gentlewoman starting to make a living, you can still open a little school; and you can easily buy a secondhand brass plate inscribed PESTALOZZIAN INSTITUTE and nail it to your door, though you have no more idea of who Pestalozzi was and what he advocated or how he did it than the manager of a hotel which began as a Hydropathic has of the water cure. Or you can buy a cheaper plate inscribed KINDERGARTEN, and imagine, or leave others to imagine, that Froebel is the governing genius of your little creche. No doubt the new brass plates are being inscribed Montessori Institute, and will be used when the Dotteressa is no longer with us by all the Mrs Pipchins and Mrs Wilfers throughout this unhappy land.

I will go further, and admit that the brass plates may not all be frauds. I will tell you that one of my friends was led to genuine love and considerable knowledge of classical literature by an Irish schoolmaster whom you would call a hedge schoolmaster (he would not be allowed to teach anything now) and that it took four years of Harrow to obliterate that knowledge and change the love into loathing. Another friend of mine who keeps a school in the suburbs, and who deeply deplores my "prejudice against schoolmasters," has offered to accept my challenge to tell his pupils that they are as free to get up and go out of the school at any moment as their parents are to get up and go out of a theatre where my plays are being performed. Even among my own schoolmasters I can recollect a few whose classes interested me, and whom I should certainly have pestered for information and instruction if I could have got into any decent human relationship with them, and if they had not been compelled by their position to defend themselves as carefully against such advances as against furtive attempts to hurt them accidentally in the football field or smash their hats with a clod from behind a wall. But these rare cases actually do more harm than good; for they encourage us to pretend that all schoolmasters are like that. Of what use is it to us that there are always somewhere two or three teachers of children whose specific genius for their occupation triumphs over our tyrannous system and even finds in it its opportunity? For that matter, it is possible, if difficult, to find a solicitor, or even a judge, who has some notion of what law means, a doctor with a glimmering of science, an officer who understands duty and discipline, and a clergyman with an inkling of religion, though there are nothing like enough of them to go round. But even the few who, like Ibsen's Mrs Solness, have "a genius for nursing the souls of little children" are like angels forced to work in prisons instead of in heaven; and even at that they are mostly underpaid and despised. That friend of mine who went from the hedge schoolmaster to Harrow once saw a schoolmaster rush from an elementary school in pursuit of a boy and strike him. My friend, not considering that the unfortunate man was probably goaded beyond endurance, smote the schoolmaster and blackened his eye. The schoolmaster appealed to the law; and my friend found himself waiting nervously in the Hammersmith Police Court to answer for his breach of the peace. In his anxiety he asked a police officer what would happen to him. "What did you do?" said the officer. "I gave a man a black eye" said my friend. "Six pounds if he was a gentleman: two pounds if he wasnt," said the constable. "He was a schoolmaster" said my friend. "Two pounds" said the officer; and two pounds it was. The blood money was paid cheerfully; and I have ever since advised elementary schoolmasters to qualify themselves in the art of self-defence, as the British Constitution expresses our national estimate of them by allowing us to blacken three of their eyes for the same price as one of an ordinary professional man. How many Froebels and Pestalozzis and Miss Masons and Doctoress Montessoris would you be likely to get on these terms even if they occurred much more frequently in nature than they actually do?

No: I cannot be put off by the news that our system would be perfect if it were worked by angels. I do not admit it even at that, just as I do not admit that if the sky fell we should all catch larks. But I do not propose to bother about a supply of specific genius which does not exist, and which, if it did exist, could operate only by at once recognizing and establishing the rights of children.

What We Do Not Teach, and Why

To my mind, a glance at the subjects now taught in schools ought to convince any reasonable person that the object of the lessons is to keep children out of mischief, and not to qualify them for their part in life as responsible citizens of a free State. It is not possible to maintain freedom in any State, no matter how perfect its original constitution, unless its publicly active citizens know a good deal of constitutional history, law, and political science, with its basis of economics. If as much pains had been taken a century ago to make us all understand Ricardo's law of rent as to learn our catechisms, the face of the world would have been changed for the better. But for that very reason the greatest care is taken to keep such beneficially subversive knowledge from us, with the result that in public life we are either place-hunters, anarchists, or sheep shepherded by wolves.

But it will be observed that these are highly controversial subjects. Now no controversial subject can be taught dogmatically. He who knows only the official side of a controversy knows less than nothing of its nature. The abler a schoolmaster is, the more dangerous he is to his pupils unless they have the fullest opportunity of hearing another equally able person do his utmost to shake his authority and convict him of error.

At present such teaching is very unpopular. It does not exist in schools; but every adult who derives his knowledge of public affairs from the newspapers can take in, at the cost of an extra halfpenny, two papers of opposite politics. Yet the ordinary man so dislikes having his mind unsettled, as he calls it, that he angrily refuses to allow a paper which dissents from his views to be brought into his house. Even at his club he resents seeing it, and excludes it if it happens to run counter to the opinions of all the members. The result is that his opinions are not worth considering. A churchman who never reads The Freethinker very soon has no more real religion than the atheist who never reads The Church Times. The attitude is the same in both cases: they want to hear nothing good of their enemies; consequently they remain enemies and suffer from bad blood all their lives; whereas men who know their opponents and understand their case, quite commonly respect and like them, and always learn something from them.

Here, again, as at so many points, we come up against the abuse of schools to keep people in ignorance and error, so that they may be incapable of successful revolt against their industrial slavery. The most important simple fundamental economic truth to impress on a child in complicated civilizations like ours is the truth that whoever consumes goods or services without producing by personal effort the equivalent of what he or she consumes, inflicts on the community precisely the same injury that a thief produces, and would, in any honest State, be treated as a thief, however full his or her pockets might be of money made by other people. The nation that first teaches its children that truth, instead of flogging them if they discover it for themselves, may have to fight all the slaves of all the other nations to begin with; but it will beat them as easily as an unburdened man with his hands free and with all his energies in full play can beat an invalid who has to carry another invalid on his back.

This, however, is not an evil produced by the denial of children's rights, nor is it inherent in the nature of schools. I mention it only because it would be folly to call for a reform of our schools without taking account of the corrupt resistance which awaits the reformer.

A word must also be said about the opposition to reform of the vested interest of the classical and coercive schoolmaster. He, poor wretch, has no other means of livelihood; and reform would leave him as a workman is now left when he is superseded by a machine. He had therefore better do what he can to get the workman compensated, so as to make the public familiar with the idea of compensation before his own turn comes.

Taboo in Schools

The suppression of economic knowledge, disastrous as it is, is quite intelligible, its corrupt motive being as clear as the motive of a burglar for concealing his jemmy from a policeman. But the other great suppression in our schools, the suppression of the subject of sex, is a case of taboo. In mankind, the lower the type, and the less cultivated the mind, the less courage there is to face important subjects objectively. The ablest and most highly cultivated people continually discuss religion, politics, and sex: it is hardly an exaggeration to say that they discuss nothing else with fully-awakened interest. Commoner and less cultivated people, even when they form societies for discussion, make a rule that politics and religion are not to be mentioned, and take it for granted that no decent person would attempt to discuss sex. The three subjects are feared because they rouse the crude passions which call for furious gratification in murder and rapine at worst, and, at best, lead to quarrels and undesirable states of consciousness.

Even when this excuse of bad manners, ill temper, and brutishness (for that is what it comes to) compels us to accept it from those adults among whom political and theological discussion does as a matter of fact lead to the drawing of knives and pistols, and sex discussion leads to obscenity, it has no application to children except as an imperative reason for training them to respect other people's opinions, and to insist on respect for their own in these as in other important matters which are equally dangerous: for example, money. And in any case there are decisive reasons; superior, like the reasons for suspending conventional reticences between doctor and patient, to all considerations of mere decorum, for giving proper instruction in the facts of sex. Those who object to it (not counting coarse people who thoughtlessly seize every opportunity of affecting and parading a fictitious delicacy) are, in effect, advocating ignorance as a safeguard against precocity. If ignorance were practicable there would be something to be said for it up to the age at which ignorance is a danger instead of a safeguard. Even as it is, it seems undesirable that any special emphasis should be given to the subject, whether by way of delicacy and poetry or too impressive warning. But the plain fact is that in refusing to allow the child to be taught by qualified unrelated elders (the parents shrink from the lesson, even when they are otherwise qualified, because their own relation to the child makes the subject impossible between them) we are virtually arranging to have our children taught by other children in guilty secrets and unclean jests. And that settles the question for all sensible people.

The dogmatic objection, the sheer instinctive taboo which rules the subject out altogether as indecent, has no age limit. It means that at no matter what age a woman consents to a proposal of marriage, she should do so in ignorance of the relation she is undertaking. When this actually happens (and apparently it does happen oftener than would seem possible) a horrible fraud is being practiced on both the man and the woman. He is led to believe that she knows what she is promising, and that he is in no danger of finding himself bound to a woman to whom he is eugenically antipathetic. She contemplates nothing but such affectionate relations as may exist between her and her nearest kinsmen, and has no knowledge of the condition which, if not foreseen, must come as an amazing revelation and a dangerous shock, ending possibly in the discovery that the marriage has been an irreparable mistake. Nothing can justify such a risk. There may be people incapable of understanding that the right to know all there is to know about oneself is a natural human right that sweeps away all the pretences of others to tamper with one's consciousness in order to produce what they choose to consider a good character. But they must here bow to the plain mischievousness of entrapping people into contracts on which the happiness of their whole lives depends without letting them know what they are undertaking.

Alleged Novelties in Modern Schools

There is just one more nuisance to be disposed of before I come to the positive side of my case. I mean the person who tells me that my schooldays belong to a bygone order of educational ideas and institutions, and that schools are not now a bit like my old school. I reply, with Sir Walter Raleigh, by calling on my soul to give this statement the lie. Some years ago I lectured in Oxford on the subject of Education. A friend to whom I mentioned my intention said, "You know nothing of modern education: schools are not now what they were when you were a boy." I immediately procured the time sheets of half a dozen modern schools, and found, as I expected, that they might all have been my old school: there was no real difference. I may mention, too, that I have visited modern schools, and observed that there is a tendency to hang printed pictures in an untidy and soulless manner on the walls, and occasionally to display on the mantel-shelf a deplorable glass case containing certain objects which might possibly, if placed in the hands of the pupils, give them some practical experience of the weight of a pound and the length of an inch. And sometimes a scoundrel who has rifled a bird's nest or killed a harmless snake encourages the children to go and do likewise by putting his victims into an imitation nest and bottle and exhibiting them as aids to "Nature study." A suggestion that Nature is worth study would certainly have staggered my schoolmasters; so perhaps I may admit a gleam of progress here. But as any child who attempted to handle these dusty objects would probably be caned, I do not attach any importance to such modernities in school furniture. The school remains what it was in my boyhood, because its real object remains what it was. And that object, I repeat, is to keep the children out of mischief: mischief meaning for the most part worrying the grown-ups.

What is to be Done?

The practical question, then, is what to do with the children. Tolerate them at home we will not. Let them run loose in the streets we dare not until our streets become safe places for children, which, to our utter shame, they are not at present, though they can hardly be worse than some homes and some schools.

The grotesque difficulty of making even a beginning was brought home to me in the little village in Hertfordshire where I write these lines by the lady of the manor, who asked me very properly what I was going to do for the village school. I did not know what to reply. As the school kept the children quiet during my working hours, I did not for the sake of my own personal convenmence want to blow it up with dynamite as I should like to blow up most schools. So I asked for guidance. "You ought to give a prize," said the lady. I asked if there was a prize for good conduct. As I expected, there was: one for the best-behaved boy and another for the best-behaved girl. On reflection I offered a handsome prize for the worst-behaved boy and girl on condition that a record should be kept of their subsequent careers and compared with the records of the best-behaved, in order to ascertain whether the school criterion of good conduct was valid out of school. My offer was refused because it would not have had the effect of encouraging the children to give as little trouble as possible, which is of course the real object of all conduct prizes in schools.

I must not pretend, then, that I have a system ready to replace all the other systems. Obstructing the way of the proper organization of childhood, as of everything else, lies our ridiculous misdistribution of the national income, with its accompanying class distinctions and imposition of snobbery on children as a necessary part of their social training. The result of our economic folly is that we are a nation of undesirable acquaintances; and the first object of all our institutions for children is segregation. If, for example, our children were set free to roam and play about as they pleased, they would have to be policed; and the first duty of the police in a State like ours would be to see that every child wore a badge indicating its class in society, and that every child seen speaking to another child with a lower-class badge, or any child wearing a higher badge than that allotted to it by, say, the College of Heralds, should immediately be skinned alive with a birch rod. It might even be insisted that girls with high-class badges should be attended by footmen, grooms, or even military escorts. In short, there is hardly any limit to the follies with which our Commercialism would infect any system that it would tolerate at all. But something like a change of heart is still possible; and since all the evils of snobbery and segregation are rampant in our schools at present we may as well make the best as the worst of them.

Children's Rights and Duties

Now let us ask what are a child's rights, and what are the rights of society over the child. Its rights, being clearly those of any other human being, are summed up in the right to live: that is, to have all the conclusive arguments that prove that it would be better dead, that it is a child of wrath, that the population is already excessive, that the pains of life are greater than its pleasures, that its sacrifice in a hospital or laboratory experiment might save millions of lives, etc. etc. etc., put out of the question, and its existence accepted as necessary and sacred, all theories to the contrary notwithstanding, whether by Calvin or Schopenhauer or Pasteur or the nearest person with a taste for infanticide. And this right to live includes, and in fact is, the right to be what the child likes and can, to do what it likes and can, to make what it likes and can, to think what it likes and can, to smash what it dislikes and can, and generally to behave in an altogether unaccountable manner within the limits imposed by the similar rights of its neighbors. And the rights of society over it clearly extend to requiring it to qualify itself to live in society without wasting other peoples time: that is, it must know the rules of the road, be able to read placards and proclamations, fill voting papers, compose and send letters and telegrams, purchase food and clothing and railway tickets for itself, count money and give and take change, and, generally, know how many beans made five. It must know some law, were it only a simple set of commandments, some political economy, agriculture enough to shut the gates of fields with cattle in them and not to trample on growing crops, sanitation enough not to defile its haunts, and religion enough to have some idea of why it is allowed its rights and why it must respect the rights of others. And the rest of its education must consist of anything else it can pick up; for beyond this society cannot go with any certainty, and indeed can only go this far rather apologetically and provisionally, as doing the best it can on very uncertain ground.

Should Children Earn their Living?

Now comes the question how far children should be asked to contribute to the support of the community. In approaching it we must put aside the considerations that now induce all humane and thoughtful political students to agitate for the uncompromising abolition of child labor under our capitalist system. It is not the least of the curses of that system that it will bequeath to future generations a mass of legislation to prevent capitalists from "using up nine generations of men in one generation," as they began by doing until they were restrained by law at the suggestion of Robert Owen, the founder of English Socialism. Most of this legislation will become an insufferable restraint upon freedom and variety of action when Capitalism goes the way of Druidic human sacrifice (a much less slaughterous institution). There is every reason why a child should not be allowed to work for commercial profit or for the support of its parents at the expense of its own future; but there is no reason whatever why a child should not do some work for its own sake and that of the community if it can be shewn that both it and the community will be the better for it.

Children's Happiness

Also it is important to put the happiness of the children rather carefully in its place, which is really not a front place. The unsympathetic, selfish, hard people who regard happiness as a very exceptional indulgence to which children are by no means entitled, though they may be allowed a very little of it on their birthdays or at Christmas, are sometimes better parents in effect than those who imagine that children are as capable of happiness as adults. Adults habitually exaggerate their own capacity in that direction grossly; yet most adults can stand an allowance of happiness that would be quite thrown away on children. The secret of being miserable is to have leisure to bother about whether you are happy or not. The cure for it is occupation, because occupation means pre-occupation; and the pre-occupied person is neither happy nor unhappy, but simply alive and active, which is pleasanter than any happiness until you are tired of it. That is why it is necessary to happiness that one should be tired. Music after dinner is pleasant: music before breakfast is so unpleasant as to be clearly unnatural. To people who are not overworked holidays are a nuisance. To people who are, and who can afford them, they are a troublesome necessity. A perpetual holiday is a good working definition of hell.

The Horror of the Perpetual Holiday

It will be said here that, on the contrary, heaven is always conceived as a perpetual holiday, and that whoever is not born to an independent income is striving for one or longing for one because it gives holidays for life. To which I reply, first, that heaven, as conventionally conceived, is a place so inane, so dull, so useless, so miserable, that nobody has ever ventured to describe a whole day in heaven, though plenty of people have described a day at the seaside; and that the genuine popular verdict on it is expressed in the proverb "Heaven for holiness and Hell for company." Second, I point out that the wretched people who have independent incomes and no useful occupation, do the most amazingly disagreeable and dangerous things to make themselves tired and hungry in the evening. When they are not involved in what they call sport, they are doing aimlessly what other people have to be paid to do: driving horses and motor cars; trying on dresses and walking up and down to shew them off; and acting as footmen and housemaids to royal personages. The sole and obvious cause of the notion that idleness is delightful and that heaven is a place where there is nothing to be done, is our school system and our industrial system. The school is a prison in which work is a punishment and a curse. In avowed prisons, hard labor, the only alleviation of a prisoner's lot, is treated as an aggravation of his punishment; and everything possible is done to intensify the prisoner's inculcated and unnatural notion that work is an evil. In industry we are overworked and underfed prisoners. Under such absurd circumstances our judgment of things becomes as perverted as our habits. If we were habitually underworked and overfed, our notion of heaven would be a place where everybody worked strenuously for twenty-four hours a day and never got anything to eat.

Once realize that a perpetual holiday is beyond human endurance, and that "Satan finds some mischief still for idle hands to do" and it will be seen that we have no right to impose a perpetual holiday on children. If we did, they would soon outdo the Labor Party in their claim for a Right to Work Bill.

In any case no child should be brought up to suppose that its food and clothes come down from heaven or are miraculously conjured from empty space by papa. Loathsome as we have made the idea of duty (like the idea of work) we must habituate children to a sense of repayable obligation to the community for what they consume and enjoy, and inculcate the repayment as a point of honor. If we did that today - and nothing but flat dishonesty prevents us from doing it - we should have no idle rich and indeed probably no rich, since there is no distinction in being rich if you have to pay scot and lot in personal effort like the working folk. Therefore, if for only half an hour a day, a child should do something serviceable to the community.

Productive work for children has the advantage that its discipline is the discipline of impersonal necessity, not that of wanton personal coercion. The eagerness of children in our industrial districts to escape from school to the factory is not caused by lighter tasks or shorter hours in the factory, nor altogether by the temptation of wages, nor even by the desire for novelty, but by the dignity of adult work, the exchange of the factitious personal tyranny of the schoolmaster, from which the grown-ups are free, for the stern but entirely dignified Laws of Life to which all flesh is subject.

University Schoolboyishness

Older children might do a good deal before beginning their collegiate education. What is the matter with our universities is that all the students are schoolboys, whereas it is of the very essence of university education that they should be men. The function of a university is not to teach things that can now be taught as well or better by University Extension lectures or by private tutors or modern correspondence classes with gramophones. We go to them to be socialized; to acquire the hall mark of communal training; to become citizens of the world instead of inmates of the enlarged rabbit hutches we call homes; to learn manners and become unchallengeable ladies and gentlemen. The social pressure which effects these changes should be that of persons who have faced the full responsibilities of adults as working members of the general community, not that of a barbarous rabble of half emancipated schoolboys and unemancipable pedants. It is true that in a reasonable state of society this outside experience would do for us very completely what the university does now so corruptly that we tolerate its bad manners only because they are better than no manners at all. But the university will always exist in some form as a community of persons desirous of pushing their culture to the highest pitch they are capable of, not as solitary students reading in seclusion, but as members of a body of individuals all pursuing culture, talking culture, thinking culture, above all, criticizing culture. If such persons are to read and talk and criticize to any purpose, they must know the world outside the university at least as well as the shopkeeper in the High Street does. And this is just what they do not know at present. You may say of them, paraphrasing Mr. Kipling, "What do they know of Plato that only Plato know?" If our universities would exclude everybody who had not earned a living by his or her own exertions for at least a couple of years, their effect would be vastly improved.

The New Laziness

The child of the future, then, if there is to be any future but one of decay, will work more or less for its living from an early age; and in doing so it will not shock anyone, provided there be no longer any reason to associate the conception of children working for their living with infants toiling in a factory for ten hours a day or boys drudging from nine to six under gas lamps in underground city offices. Lads and lasses in their teens will probably be able to produce as much as the most expensive person now costs in his own person (it is retinue that eats up the big income) without working too hard or too long for quite as much happiness as they can enjoy. The question to be balanced then will be, not how soon people should be put to work, but how soon they should be released from any obligation of the kind. A life's work is like a day's work: it can begin early and leave off early or begin late and leave off late, or, as with us, begin too early and never leave off at all, obviously the worst of all possible plans. In any event we must finally reckon work, not as the curse our schools and prisons and capitalist profit factories make it seem today, but as a prime necessity of a tolerable existence. And if we cannot devise fresh wants as fast as we develop the means of supplying them, there will come a scarcity of the needed, cut-and-dried, appointed work that is always ready to everybody's hand. It may have to be shared out among people all of whom want more of it. And then a new sort of laziness will become the bugbear of society: the laziness that refuses to face the mental toil and adventure of making work by inventing new ideas or extending the domain of knowledge, and insists on a ready-made routine. It may come to forcing people to retire before they are willing to make way for younger ones: that is, to driving all persons of a certain age out of industry, leaving them to find something experimental to occupy them on pain of perpetual holiday. Men will then try to spend twenty thousand a year for the sake of having to earn it. Instead of being what we are now, the cheapest and nastiest of the animals, we shall be the costliest, most fastidious, and best bred. In short, there is no end to the astonishing things that may happen when the curse of Adam becomes first a blessing and then an incurable habit. And in that day we must not grudge children their share of it.

The Infinite School Task

The question of children's work, however, is only a question of what the child ought to do for the community. How highly it should qualify itself is another matter. But most of the difficulty of inducing children to learn would disappear if our demands became not only definite but finite. When learning is only an excuse for imprisonment, it is an instrument of torture which becomes more painful the more progress is made. Thus when you have forced a child to learn the Church Catechism, a document profound beyond the comprehension of most adults, you are sometimes at a standstill for something else to teach; and you therefore keep the wretched child repeating its catechism again and again until you hit on the plan of making it learn instalments of Bible verses, preferably from the book of Numbers. But as it is less trouble to set a lesson that you know yourself, there is a tendency to keep repeating the already learnt lesson rather than break new ground. At school I began with a fairly complete knowledge of Latin grammar in the childish sense of being able to repeat all the paradigms; and I was kept at this, or rather kept in a class where the master never asked me to do it because he knew I could, and therefore devoted himself to trapping the boys who could not, until I finally forgot most of it. But when progress took place, what did it mean? First it meant Caesar, with the foreknowledge that to master

Caesar meant only being set at Virgil, with the culminating horror of Greek and Homer in reserve at the end of that. I preferred Caesar, because his statement that Gaul is divided into three parts, though neither interesting nor true, was the only Latin sentence I could translate at sight: therefore the longer we stuck at Caesar the better I was pleased. Just so do less classically educated children see nothing in the mastery of addition but the beginning of subtraction, and so on through multiplication and division and fractions, with the black cloud of algebra on the horizon. And if a boy rushes through all that, there is always the calculus to fall back on, unless indeed you insist on his learning music, and proceed to hit him if he cannot tell you the year Beethoven was born.

A child has a right to finality as regards its compulsory lessons. Also as regards physical training. At present it is assumed that the schoolmaster has a right to force every child into an attempt to become Porson and Bentley, Leibnitz and Newton, all rolled into one. This is the tradition of the oldest grammar schools. In our times an even more horrible and cynical claim has been made for the right to drive boys through compulsory games in the playing fields until they are too much exhausted physically to do anything but drop off to sleep. This is supposed to protect them from vice; but as it also protects them from poetry, literature, music, meditation and prayer, it may be dismissed with the obvious remark that if boarding schools are places whose keepers are driven to such monstrous measures lest more abominable things should happen, then the sooner boarding schools are violently abolished the better. It is true that society may make physical claims on the child as well as mental ones: the child must learn to walk, to use a knife and fork, to swim, to ride a bicycle, to acquire sufficient power of self-defence to make an attack on it an arduous and uncertain enterprise, perhaps to fly. What as a matter of common-sense it clearly has not a right to do is to make this an excuse for keeping the child slaving for ten hours at physical exercises on the ground that it is not yet as dexterous as Cinquevalli and as strong as Sandow.

The Rewards and Risks of Knowledge

In a word, we have no right to insist on educating a child; for its education can end only with its life and will not even then be complete. Compulsory completion of education is the last folly of a rotten and desperate civilization. It is the rattle in its throat before dissolution. All we can fairly do is to prescribe certain definite acquirements and accomplishments as qualifications for certain employments; and to secure them, not by the ridiculous method of inflicting injuries on the persons who have not yet mastered them, but by attaching certain privileges (not pecuniary) to the employments.

Most acquirements carry their own privileges with them. Thus a baby has to be pretty closely guarded and imprisoned because it cannot take care of itself. It has even to be carried about (the most complete conceivable infringement of its liberty) until it can walk. But nobody goes on carrying children after they can walk lest they should walk into mischief, though Arab boys make their sisters carry them, as our own spoiled children sometimes make their nurses, out of mere laziness, because sisters in the East and nurses in the West are kept in servitude. But in a society of equals (the only reasonable and permanently possible sort of society) children are in much greater danger of acquiring bandy legs through being left to walk before they are strong enough than of being carried when they are well able to walk. Anyhow, freedom of movement in a nursery is the reward of learning to walk; and in precisely the same way freedom of movement in a city is the reward of learning how to read public notices, and to count and use money. The consequences are of course much larger than the mere ability to read the name of a street or the number of a railway platform and the destination of a train. When you enable a child to read these, you also enable it to read this preface, to the utter destruction, you may quite possibly think, of its morals and docility. You also expose it to the danger of being run over by taxicabs and trains. The moral and physical risks of education are enormous: every new power a child acquires, from speaking, walking, and co-ordinating its vision, to conquering continents and founding religions, opens up immense new possibilities of mischief. Teach a child to write and you teach it how to forge: teach it to speak and you teach it how to lie: teach it to walk and you teach it how to kick its mother to death.

The great problem of slavery for those whose aim is to maintain it is the problem of reconciling the efficiency of the slave with the helplessness that keeps him in servitude; and this problem is fortunately not completely soluble; for it is not in fact found possible for a duke to treat his solicitor or his doctor as he treats his laborers, though they are all equally his slaves: the laborer being in fact less dependent on his favor than the professional man. Hence it is that men come to resent, of all things, protection, because it so often means restriction of their liberty lest they should make a bad use of it. If there are dangerous precipices about, it is much easier and cheaper to forbid people to walk near the edge than to put up an effective fence: that is why both legislators and parents and the paid deputies of parents are always inhibiting and prohibiting and punishing and scolding and laming and cramping and delaying progress and growth instead of making the dangerous places as safe as possible and then boldly taking and allowing others to take the irreducible minimum of risk.

English Physical Hardihood and Spiritual Cowardice

It is easier to convert most people to the need for allowing their children to run physical risks than moral ones. I can remember a relative of mine who, when I was a small child, unused to horses and very much afraid of them, insisted on putting me on a rather rumbustious pony with little spurs on my heels (knowing that in my agitation I would use them unconsciously), and being enormously amused at my terrors. Yet when that same lady discovered that I had found a copy of The Arabian Nights and was devouring it with avidity, she was horrified, and hid it away from me lest it should break my soul as the pony might have broken my neck. This way of producing hardy bodies and timid souls is so common in country houses that you may spend hours in them listening to stories of broken collar bones, broken backs, and broken necks without coming upon a single spiritual adventure or daring thought.

But whether the risks to which liberty exposes us are moral or physical our right to liberty involves the right to run them. A man who is not free to risk his neck as an aviator or his soul as a heretic is not free at all; and the right to liberty begins, not at the age of 21 years but of 21 seconds.

The Risks of Ignorance and Weakness

The difficulty with children is that they need protection from risks they are too young to understand, and attacks they can neither avoid nor resist. You may on academic grounds allow a child to snatch glowing coals from the fire once. You will not do it twice. The risks of liberty we must let everyone take; but the risks of ignorance and self-helplessness are another matter. Not only children but adults need protection from them. At present adults are often exposed to risks outside their knowledge or beyond their comprehension or powers of resistance or foresight: for example, we have to look on every day at marriages or financial speculations that may involve far worse consequences than burnt fingers. And just as it is part of the business of adults to protect children, to feed them, clothe them, shelter them, and shift for them in all sorts of ways until they are able to shift for themselves, it is coming more and more to be seen that this is true not only of the relation between adults and children, but between adults and adults. We shall not always look on indifferently at foolish marriages and financial speculations, nor allow dead men to control live communities by ridiculous wills and living heirs to squander and ruin great estates, nor tolerate a hundred other absurd liberties that we allow today because we are too lazy to find out the proper way to interfere. But the interference must be regulated by some theory of the individual's rights. Though the right to live is absolute, it is not unconditional. If a man is unbearably mischievous, he must be killed. This is a mere matter of necessity, like the killing of a man-eating tiger in a nursery, a venomous snake in the garden, or a fox in the poultry yard. No society could be constructed on the assumption that such extermination is a violation of the creature's right to live, and therefore must not be allowed. And then at once arises the danger into which morality has led us: the danger of persecution. One Christian spreading his doctrines may seem more mischievous than a dozen thieves: throw him therefore to the lions. A lying or disobedient child may corrupt a whole generation and make human Society impossible: therefore thrash the vice out of him. And so on until our whole system of abortion, intimidation, tyranny, cruelty and the rest is in full swing again.

The Common Sense of Toleration

The real safeguard against this is the dogma of Toleration. I need not here repeat the compact treatise on it which I prepared for the Joint Committee on the Censorship of Stage Plays, and prefixed to The Shewing Up of Blanco Posnet. It must suffice now to say that the present must not attempt to schoolmaster the future by pretending to know good from evil in tendency, or protect citizens against shocks to their opinions and convictions, moral, political or religious: in other words it must not persecute doctrines of any kind, or what is called bad taste, and must insist on all persons facing such shocks as they face frosty weather or any of the other disagreeable, dangerous, or bracing incidents of freedom. The expediency of Toleration has been forced on us by the fact that progressive enlightenment depends on a fair hearing for doctrines which at first appear seditious, blasphemous, and immoral, and which deeply shock people who never think originally, thought being with them merely a habit and an echo. The deeper ground for Toleration is the nature of creation, which, as we now know, proceeds by evolution. Evolution finds its way by experiment; and this finding of the way varies according to the stage of development reached, from the blindest groping along the line of least resistance to intellectual speculation, with its practical sequel of hypothesis and experimental verification; or to observation, induction, and deduction; or even into so rapid and intuitive an integration of all these processes in a single brain that we get the inspired guess of the man of genius and the desperate resolution of the teacher of new truths who is first slain as a blasphemous apostate and then worshipped as a prophet.

Here the law for the child is the same as for the adult. The high priest must not rend his garments and cry "Crucify him" when he is shocked: the atheist must not clamor for the suppression of Law's Serious Call because it has for two centuries destroyed the natural happiness of innumerable unfortunate children by persuading their parents that it is their religious duty to be miserable. It, and the Sermon on the Mount, and Machiavelli's Prince, and La Rochefoucauld's maxims, and Hymns Ancient and Modern, and De Glanville's apologue, and Dr. Watts's rhymes, and Nietzsche's Gay Science, and Ingersoll's Mistakes of Moses, and the speeches and pamphlets of the people who want us to make war on Germany, and the Noodle's Orations and articles of our politicians and journalists, must all be tolerated not only because any of them may for all we know be on the right track but because it is in the conflict of opinion that we win knowledge and wisdom. However terrible the wounds suffered in that conflict, they are better than the barren peace of death that follows when all the combatants are slaughtered or bound hand and foot.

The difficulty at present is that though this necessity for Toleration is a law of political science as well established as the law of gravitation, our rulers are never taught political science: on the contrary, they are taught in school that the master tolerates nothing that is disagreeable to him; that ruling is simply being master; and that the master's method is the method of violent punishment. And our citizens, all school taught, are walking in the same darkness. As I write these lines the Home Secretary is explaining that a man who has been imprisoned for blasphemy must not be released because his remarks were painful to the feelings of his pious fellow townsmen. Now it happens that this very Home Secretary has driven many thousands of his fellow citizens almost beside themselves by the crudity of his notions of government, and his simple inability to understand why he should not use and make laws to torment and subdue people who do not happen to agree with him. In a word, he is not a politician, but a grown-up schoolboy who has at last got a cane in his hand. And as all the rest of us are in the same condition (except as to command of the cane) the only objection made to his proceedings takes the shape of clamorous demands that he should be caned instead of being allowed to cane other people.

The Sin of Athanasius

It seems hopeless. Anarchists are tempted to preach a violent and implacable resistance to all law as the only remedy; and the result of that speedily is that people welcome any tyranny that will rescue them from chaos. But there is really no need to choose between anarchy and tyranny. A quite reasonable state of things is practicable if we proceed on human assumptions and not on academic ones. If adults will frankly give up their claim to know better than children what the purposes of the Life Force are, and treat the child as an experiment like themselves, and possibly a more successful one, and at the same time relinquish their monstrous parental claims to personal private property in children, the rest must be left to common sense. It is our attitude, our religion, that is wrong. A good beginning might be made by enacting that any person dictating a piece of conduct to a child or to anyone else as the will of God, or as absolutely right, should be dealt with as a blasphemer: as, indeed, guilty of the unpardonable sin against the Holy Ghost. If the penalty were death, it would rid us at once of that scourge of humanity, the amateur Pope. As an Irish Protestant, I raise the cry of No Popery with hereditary zest. We are overrun with Popes. From curates and governesses, who may claim a sort of professional standing, to parents and uncles and nurserymaids and school teachers and wiseacres generally, there are scores of thousands of human insects groping through our darkness by the feeble phosphorescence of their own tails, yet ready at a moment's notice to reveal the will of God on every possible subject; to explain how and why the universe was made (in my youth they added the exact date) and the circumstances under which it will cease to exist; to lay down precise rules of right and wrong conduct; to discriminate infallibly between virtuous and vicious character; and all this with such certainty that they are prepared to visit all the rigors of the law, and all the ruinous penalties of social ostracism on people, however harmless their actions maybe who venture to laugh at their monstrous conceit or to pay their assumptions the extravagant compliment of criticizing them. As to children, who shall say what canings and birchings and terrifyings and threats of hell fire and impositions and humiliations and petty imprisonings and sendings to bed and standing in corners and the like they have suffered because their parents and guardians and teachers knew everything so much better than Socrates or Solon?

It is this ignorant uppishness that does the mischief. A stranger on the planet might expect that its grotesque absurdity would provoke enough ridicule to cure it; but unfortunately quite the contrary happens. Just as our ill health delivers us into the hands of medical quacks and creates a passionate demand for impudent pretences that doctors can cure the diseases they themselves die of daily, so our ignorance and helplessness set us clamoring for spiritual and moral quacks who pretend that they can save our souls from their own damnation. If a doctor were to say to his patients, "I am familiar with your symptoms, because I have seen other people in your condition; and I will bring the very little knowledge we have to your treatment; but except in that very shallow sense I dont know what is the matter with you; and I cant undertake to cure you," he would be a lost man professionally; and if a clergyman, on being called on to award a prize for good conduct in the village school, were to say, "I am afraid I cannot say who is the best-behaved child, because I really do not know what good conduct is; but I will gladly take the teacher's word as to which child has caused least inconvenience," he would probably be unfrocked, if not excommunicated. And yet no honest and intellectually capable doctor or parson can say more. Clearly it would not be wise of the doctor to say it, because optimistic lies have such immense therapeutic value that a doctor who cannot tell them convincingly has mistaken his profession. And a clergyman who is not prepared to lay down the law dogmatically will not be of much use in a village school, though it behoves him all the more to be very careful what law he lays down. But unless both the clergyman and the doctor are in the attitude expressed by these speeches they are not fit for their work. The man who believes that he has more than a provisional hypothesis to go upon is a born fool. He may have to act vigorously on it. The world has no use for the Agnostic who wont believe anything because anything might be false, and wont deny anything because anything might be true. But there is a wide difference between saying, "I believe this; and I am going to act on it," or, "I dont believe it; and I wont act on it," and saying, "It is true; and it is my duty and yours to act on it," or, "It is false; and it is my duty and yours to refuse to act on it." The difference is as great as that between the Apostles' Creed and the Athanasian Creed. When you repeat the Apostles' Creed you affirm that you believe certain things. There you are clearly within your rights. When you repeat the Athanasian Creed, you affirm that certain things are so, and that anybody who doubts that they are so cannot be saved. And this is simply a piece of impudence on your part, as you know nothing about it except that as good men as you have never heard of your creed. The apostolic attitude is a desire to convert others to our beliefs for the sake of sympathy and light: the Athanasian attitude is a desire to murder people who dont agree with us. I am sufficient of an Athanasian to advocate a law for the speedy execution of all Athanasians, because they violate the fundamental proposition of my creed, which is, I repeat, that all living creatures are experiments. The precise formula for the Superman, ci-devant The Just Man Made Perfect, has not yet been discovered. Until it is, every birth is an experiment in the Great Research which is being conducted by the Life Force to discover that formula.

The Experiment Experimenting

And now all the modern schoolmaster abortionists will rise up beaming, and say, "We quite agree. We regard every child in our school as a subject for experiment. We are always experimenting with them. We challenge the experimental test for our system. We are continually guided by our experience in our great work of moulding the character of our future citizens, etc. etc. etc." I am sorry to seem irreconcilable; but it is the Life Force that has to make the experiment and not the schoolmaster; and the Life Force for the child's purpose is in the child and not in the schoolmaster. The schoolmaster is another experiment; and a laboratory in which all the experiments began experimenting on one another would not produce intelligible results. I admit, however, that if my schoolmasters had treated me as an experiment of the Life Force: that is, if they had set me free to do as I liked subject only to my political rights and theirs, they could not have watched the experiment very long, because the first result would have been a rapid movement on my part in the direction of the door, and my disappearance there-through.

It may be worth inquiring where I should have gone to. I should say that practically every time I should have gone to a much more educational place. I should have gone into the country, or into the sea, or into the

National Gallery, or to hear a band if there was one, or to any library where there were no schoolbooks. I should have read very dry and difficult books: for example, though nothing would have induced me to read the budget of stupid party lies that served as a text-book of history in school, I remember reading Robertson's Charles V. and his history of Scotland from end to end most laboriously. Once, stung by the airs of a schoolfellow who alleged that he had read Locke On The Human Understanding, I attempted to read the Bible straight through, and actually got to the Pauline Epistles before I broke down in disgust at what seemed to me their inveterate crookedness of mind. If there had been a school where children were really free, I should have had to be driven out of it for the sake of my health by the teachers; for the children to whom a literary education can be of any use are insatiable: they will read and study far more than is good for them. In fact the real difficulty is to prevent them from wasting their time by reading for the sake of reading and studying for the sake of studying, instead of taking some trouble to find out what they really like and are capable of doing some good at. Some silly person will probably interrupt me here with the remark that many children have no appetite for a literary education at all, and would never open a book if they were not forced to. I have known many such persons who have been forced to the point of obtaining University degrees. And for all the effect their literary exercises has left on them they might just as well have been put on the treadmill. In fact they are actually less literate than the treadmill would have left them; for they might by chance have picked up and dipped into a volume of Shakespear or a translation of Homer if they had not been driven to loathe every famous name in literature. I should probably know as much Latin as

French, if Latin had not been made the excuse for my school imprisonment and degradation.

Why We Loathe Learning and Love Sport

If we are to discuss the importance of art, learning, and intellectual culture, the first thing we have to recognize is that we have very little of them at present; and that this little has not been produced by compulsory education: nay, that the scarcity is unnatural and has been produced by the violent exclusion of art and artists from schools. On the other hand we have quite a considerable degree of bodily culture: indeed there is a continual outcry against the sacrifice of mental accomplishments to athletics. In other words a sacrifice of the professed object of compulsory education to the real object of voluntary education. It is assumed that this means that people prefer bodily to mental culture; but may it not mean that they prefer liberty and satisfaction to coercion and privation. Why is it that people who have been taught Shakespear as a school subject loathe his plays and cannot by any means be persuaded ever to open his works after they escape from school, whereas there is still, 300 years after his death, a wide and steady sale for his works to people who read his plays as plays, and not as task work? If Shakespear, or for that matter, Newton and Leibnitz, are allowed to find their readers and students they will find them. If their works are annotated and paraphrased by dullards, and the annotations and paraphrases forced on all young people by imprisonment and flogging and scolding, there will not be a single man of letters or higher mathematician the more in the country: on the contrary there will be less, as so many potential lovers of literature and mathematics will have been incurably prejudiced against them. Everyone who is conversant with the class in which child imprisonment and compulsory schooling is carried out to the final extremity of the university degree knows that its scholastic culture is a sham; that it knows little about literature or art and a great deal about point-to-point races; and that the village cobbler, who has never read a page of Plato, and is admittedly a dangerously ignorant man politically, is nevertheless a Socrates compared to the classically educated gentlemen who discuss politics in country houses at election time (and at no other time) after their day's earnest and skilful shooting. Think of the years and years of weary torment the women of the piano-possessing class have been forced to spend over the keyboard, fingering scales. How many of them could be bribed to attend a pianoforte recital by a great player, though they will rise from sick beds rather than miss Ascot or Goodwood?

Another familiar fact that teaches the same lesson is that many women who have voluntarily attained a high degree of culture cannot add up their own housekeeping books, though their education in simple arithmetic was compulsory, whereas their higher education has been wholly voluntary. Everywhere we find the same result. The imprisonment, the beating, the taming and laming, the breaking of young spirits, the arrest of development, the atrophy of all inhibitive power except the power of fear, are real: the education is sham. Those who have been taught most know least.

Antichrist

Among the worst effects of the unnatural segregation of children in schools and the equally unnatural constant association of them with adults in the family is the utter defeat of the vital element in Christianity. Christ stands in the world for that intuition of the highest humanity that we, being members one of another, must not complain, must not scold, must not strike, nor revile nor persecute nor revenge nor punish. Now family life and school life are, as far as the moral training of children is concerned, nothing but the deliberate inculcation of a routine of complaint, scolding, punishment, persecution, and revenge as the natural and only possible way of dealing with evil or inconvenience. "Aint nobody to be whopped for this here?" exclaimed Sam Weller when he saw his employer's name written up on a stage coach, and conceived the phenomenon as an insult which reflected on himself. This exclamation of Sam Weller is at once the negation of Christianity and the beginning and the end of current morality; and so it will remain as long as the family and the school persist as we know them: that is, as long as the rights of children are so utterly denied that nobody will even take the trouble to ascertain what they are, and coming of age is like the turning of a convict into the street after twenty-one years penal servitude. Indeed it is worse; for the convict may have learnt before his conviction how to live in freedom and may remember how to set about it, however lamed his powers of freedom may have become through disuse; but the child knows no other way of life but the slave's way. Born free, as Rousseau says, he has been laid hands on by slaves from the moment of his birth and brought up as a slave. How is he, when he is at last set free, to be anything else than the slave he actually is, clamoring for war, for the lash, for police, prisons, and scaffolds in a wild panic of delusion that without these things he is lost. The grown-up Englishman is to the end of his days a badly brought-up child, beyond belief quarrelsome, petulant, selfish, destructive, and cowardly: afraid that the Germans will come and enslave him; that the burglar will come and rob him; that the bicycle or motor car will run over him; that the smallpox will attack him; and that the devil will run away with him and empty him out like a sack of coals on a blazing fire unless his nurse or his parents or his schoolmaster or his bishop or his judge or his army or his navy will do something to frighten these bad things away. And this Englishman, without the moral courage of a louse, will risk his neck for fun fifty times every winter in the hunting field, and at Badajos sieges and the like will ram his head into a hole bristling with sword blades rather than be beaten in the one department in which he has been brought up to consult his own honor. As a Sportsman (and war is fundamentally the sport of hunting and fighting the most dangerous of the beasts of prey) he feels free. He will tell you himself that the true sportsman is never a snob, a coward, a duffer, a cheat, a thief, or a liar. Curious, is it not, that he has not the same confidence in other sorts of man?

And even sport is losing its freedom. Soon everybody will be schooled, mentally and physically, from the cradle to the end of the term of adult compulsory military service, and finally of compulsory civil service lasting until the age of superannuation. Always more schooling, more compulsion. We are to be cured by an excess of the dose that has poisoned us. Satan is to cast out Satan.

Under the Whip

Clearly this will not do. We must reconcile education with liberty. We must find out some means of making men workers and, if need be, warriors, without making them slaves. We must cultivate the noble virtues that have their root in pride. Now no schoolmaster will teach these any more than a prison governor will teach his prisoners how to mutiny and escape. Self-preservation forces him to break the spirit that revolts against him, and to inculcate submission, even to obscene assault, as a duty. A bishop once had the hardihood to say that he would rather see England free than England sober. Nobody has yet dared to say that he would rather see an England of ignoramuses than an England of cowards and slaves. And if anyone did, it would be necessary to point out that the antithesis is not a practical one, as we have got at present an England of ignoramuses who are also cowards and slaves, and extremely proud of it at that, because in school they are taught to submit, with what they ridiculously call Oriental fatalism (as if any Oriental has ever submitted more helplessly and sheepishly to robbery and oppression than we Occidentals do), to be driven day after day into compounds and set to the tasks they loathe by the men they hate and fear, as if this were the inevitable destiny of mankind. And naturally, when they grow up, they helplessly exchange the prison of the school for the prison of the mine or the workshop or the office, and drudge along stupidly and miserably, with just enough gregarious instinct to turn furiously on any intelligent person who proposes a change. It would be quite easy to make England a paradise, according to our present ideas, in a few years. There is no mystery about it: the way has been pointed out over and over again. The difficulty is not the way but the will. And we have no will because the first thing done with us in childhood was to break our will. Can anything be more disgusting than the spectacle of a nation reading the biography of Gladstone and gloating over the account of how he was flogged at Eton, two of his schoolfellows being compelled to hold him down whilst he was flogged. Not long ago a public body in England had to deal with the case of a schoolmaster who, conceiving himself insulted by the smoking of a cigaret against his orders by a pupil eighteen years old, proposed to flog him publicly as a satisfaction to what he called his honor and authority. I had intended to give the particulars of this ease, but find the drudgery of repeating such stuff too sickening, and the effect unjust to a man who was doing only what others all over the country were doing as part of the established routine of what is called education. The astounding part of it was the manner in which the person to whom this outrage on decency seemed quite proper and natural claimed to be a functionary of high character, and had his claim allowed. In Japan he would hardly have been allowed the privilege of committing suicide. What is to be said of a profession in which such obscenities are made points of honor, or of institutions in which they are an accepted part of the daily routine? Wholesome people would not argue about the taste of such nastinesses: they would spit them out; but we are tainted with flagellomania from our childhood. When will we realize that the fact that we can become accustomed to anything, however disgusting at first, makes it necessary for us to examine carefully everything we have become accustomed to? Before motor cars became common, necessity had accustomed us to a foulness in our streets which would have horrified us had the street been our drawing-room carpet. Before long we shall be as particular about our streets as we now are about our carpets; and their condition in the nineteenth century will become as forgotten and incredible as the condition of the corridors of palaces and the courts of castles was as late as the eighteenth century. This foulness, we can plead, was imposed on us as a necessity by the use of horses and of huge retinues; but flogging has never been so imposed: it has always been a vice, craved for on any pretext by those depraved by it. Boys were flogged when criminals were hanged, to impress the awful warning on them. Boys were flogged at boundaries, to impress the boundaries on their memory. Other methods and other punishments were always available: the choice of this one betrayed the sensual impulse which makes the practice an abomination. But when its viciousness made it customary, it was practised and tolerated on all hands by people who were innocent of anything worse than stupidity, ill temper, and inability to discover other methods of maintaining order than those they had always seen practised and approved of. From children and animals it extended to slaves and criminals. In the days of Moses it was limited to 39 lashes. In the early nineteenth century it had become an open madness: soldiers were sentenced to a thousand lashes for trifling offences, with the result (among others less mentionable) that the Iron Duke of Wellington complained that it was impossible to get an order obeyed in the British army except in two or three crack regiments. Such frantic excesses of this disgusting neurosis provoked a reaction against it; but the clamor for it by depraved persons never ceased, and was tolerated by a nation trained to it from childhood in the schools until last year (1913), when in what must be described as a paroxysm of sexual excitement provoked by the agitation concerning the White Slave Traffic (the purely commercial nature of which I was prevented from exposing on the stage by the Censorship twenty years ago) the Government yielded to an outcry for flagellation led by the Archbishop of Canterbury, and passed an Act under which a judge can sentence a man to be flogged to the utmost extremity with any instrument usable for such a purpose that he cares to prescribe. Such an Act is not a legislative phenomenon but a psychopathic one. Its effect on the White Slave Traffic was, of course, to distract public attention from its real cause and from the people who really profit by it to imaginary "foreign scoundrels," and to secure a monopoly of its organization for women.

And all this evil is made possible by the schoolmaster with his cane and birch, by the parents getting rid as best they can of the nuisance of children making noise and mischief in the house, and by the denial to children of the elementary rights of human beings.

The first man who enslaved and "broke in" an animal with a whip would have invented the explosion engine instead could he have foreseen the curse he was laying on his race. For men and women learnt thereby to enslave and break in their children by the same means. These children, grown up, knew no other methods of training. Finally the evil that was done for gain by the greedy was refined on and done for pleasure by the lustful. Flogging has become a pleasure purchasable in our streets, and inhibition a grown-up habit that children play at. "Go and see what baby is doing; and tell him he mustnt" is the last word of the nursery; and the grimmest aspect of it is that it was first formulated by a comic paper as a capital joke.

Technical Instruction

Technical instruction tempts to violence (as a short cut) more than liberal education. The sailor in Mr Rudyard Kipling's Captains Courageous, teaching the boy the names of the ship's tackle with a rope's end, does not disgust us as our schoolmasters do, especially as the boy was a spoiled boy. But an unspoiled boy would not have needed that drastic medicine. Technical training may be as tedious as learning to skate or to play the piano or violin; but it is the price one must pay to achieve certain desirable results or necessary ends. It is a monstrous thing to force a child to learn Latin or Greek or mathematics on the ground that they are an indispensable gymnastic for the mental powers. It would be monstrous even if it were true; for there is no labor that might not be imposed on a child or an adult on the same pretext; but as a glance at the average products of our public school and university education shews that it is not true, it need not trouble us. But it is a fact that ignorance of Latin and Greek and mathematics closes certain careers to men (I do not mean artificial, unnecessary, noxious careers like those of the commercial schoolmaster). Languages, even dead ones, have their uses; and, as it seems to many of us, mathematics have their uses. They will always be learned by people who want to learn them; and people will always want to learn them as long as they are of any importance in life: indeed the want will survive their importance: superstition is nowhere stronger than in the field of obsolete acquirements. And they will never be learnt fruitfully by people who do not want to learn them either for their own sake or for use in necessary work. There is no harder schoolmaster than experience; and yet experience fails to teach where there is no desire to learn.

Still, one must not begin to apply this generalization too early. And this brings me to an important factor in the case: the factor of evolution.

Docility and Dependence

If anyone, impressed by my view that the rights of a child are precisely those of an adult, proceeds to treat a child as if it were an adult, he (or she) will find that though the plan will work much better at some points than the usual plan, at others it will not work at all; and this discovery may provoke him to turn back from the whole conception of children's rights with a jest at the expense of bachelors' and old maids' children. In dealing with children what is needed is not logic but sense. There is no logical reason why young persons should be allowed greater control of their property the day after they are twenty-one than the day before it. There is no logical reason why I, who strongly object to an adult standing over a boy of ten with a Latin grammar, and saying, "you must learn this, whether you want to or not," should nevertheless be quite prepared to stand over a boy of five with the multiplication table or a copy book or a code of elementary good manners, and practice on his docility to make him learn them. And there is no logical reason why I should do for a child a great many little offices, some of them troublesome and disagreeable, which I should not do for a boy twice its age, or support a boy or girl when I would unhesitatingly throw an adult on his own resources. But there are practical reasons, and sensible reasons, and affectionate reasons for all these illogicalities. Children do not want to be treated altogether as adults: such treatment terrifies them and over-burdens them with responsibility. In truth, very few adults care to be called on for independence and originality: they also are bewildered and terrified in the absence of precedents and precepts and commandments; but modern Democracy allows them a sanctioning and cancelling power if they are capable of using it, which children are not. To treat a child wholly as an adult would be to mock and destroy it. Infantile docility and juvenile dependence are, like death, a product of Natural Selection; and though there is no viler crime than to abuse them, yet there is no greater cruelty than to ignore them. I have complained sufficiently of what I suffered through the process of assault, imprisonment, and compulsory lessons that taught me nothing, which are called my schooling. But I could say a good deal also about the things I was not taught and should have been taught, not to mention the things I was allowed to do which I should not have been allowed to do. I have no recollection of being taught to read or write; so I presume I was born with both faculties; but many people seem to have bitter recollections of being forced reluctantly to acquire them. And though I have the uttermost contempt for a teacher so ill mannered and incompetent as to be unable to make a child learn to read and write without also making it cry, still I am prepared to admit that I had rather have been compelled to learn to read and write with tears by an incompetent and ill mannered person than left in ignorance. Reading, writing, and enough arithmetic to use money honestly and accurately, together with the rudiments of law and order, become necessary conditions of a child's liberty before it can appreciate the importance of its liberty, or foresee that these accomplishments are worth acquiring. Nature has provided for this by evolving the instinct of docility. Children are very docile: they have a sound intuition that they must do what they are told or perish. And adults have an intuition, equally sound, that they must take advantage of this docility to teach children how to live properly or the children will not survive. The difficulty is to know where to stop. To illustrate this, let us consider the main danger of childish docility and parental officiousness.

The Abuse of Docility

Docility may survive as a lazy habit long after it has ceased to be a beneficial instinct. If you catch a child when it is young enough to be instinctively docile, and keep it in a condition of unremitted tutelage under the nurserymaid, the governess, the preparatory school, the secondary school, and the university, until it is an adult, you will produce, not a self-reliant, free, fully matured human being, but a grown-up schoolboy or schoolgirl, capable of nothing in the way of original or independent action except outbursts of naughtiness in the women and blackguardism in the men. That is exactly what we get at present in our rich and consequently governing classes: they pass from juvenility to senility without ever touching maturity except in body. The classes which cannot afford this sustained tutelage are notably more self-reliant and grown-up: an office boy of fifteen is often more of a man than a university student of twenty. Unfortunately this precocity is disabled by poverty, ignorance, narrowness, and a hideous power of living without art or love or beauty and being rather proud of it. The poor never escape from servitude: their docility is preserved by their slavery. And so all become the prey of the greedy, the selfish, the domineering, the unscrupulous, the predatory. If here and there an individual refuses to be docile, ten docile persons will beat him or lock him up or shoot him or hang him at the bidding of his oppressors and their own. The crux of the whole difficulty about parents, schoolmasters, priests, absolute monarchs, and despots of every sort, is the tendency to abuse natural docility. A nation should always be healthily rebellious; but the king or prime minister has yet to be found who will make trouble by cultivating that side of the national spirit. A child should begin to assert itself early, and shift for itself more and more not only in washing and dressing itself, but in opinions and conduct; yet as nothing is so exasperating and so unlovable as an uppish child, it is useless to expect parents and schoolmasters to inculcate this uppishness. Such unamiable precepts as Always contradict an authoritative statement, Always return a blow, Never lose a chance of a good fight, When you are scolded for a mistake ask the person who scolds you whether he or she supposes you did it on purpose, and follow the question with a blow or an insult or some other unmistakable expression of resentment, Remember that the progress of the world depends on your knowing better than your elders, are just as important as those of The Sermon on the Mount; but no one has yet seen them written up in letters of gold in a schoolroom or nursery. The child is taught to be kind, to be respectful, to be quiet, not to answer back, to be truthful when its elders want to find out anything from it, to lie when the truth would shock or hurt its elders, to be above all things obedient, and to be seen and not heard. Here we have two sets of precepts, each warranted to spoil a child hopelessly if the other be omitted. Unfortunately we do not allow fair play between them. The rebellious, intractable, aggressive, selfish set provoke a corrective resistance, and do not pretend to high moral or religious sanctions; and they are never urged by grown-up people on young people. They are therefore more in danger of neglect or suppression than the other set, which have all the adults, all the laws, all the religions on their side. How is the child to be secured its due share of both bodies of doctrine?

The Schoolboy and the Homeboy

In practice what happens is that parents notice that boys brought up at home become mollycoddles, or prigs, or duffers, unable to take care of themselves. They see that boys should learn to rough it a little and to mix with children of their own age. This is natural enough. When you have preached at and punished a boy until he is a moral cripple, you are as much hampered by him as by a physical cripple; and as you do not intend to have him on your hands all your life, and are generally rather impatient for the day when he will earn his own living and leave you to attend to yourself, you sooner or later begin to talk to him about the need for self-reliance, learning to think, and so forth, with the result that your victim, bewildered by your inconsistency, concludes that there is no use trying to please you, and falls into an attitude of sulky resentment. Which is an additional inducement to pack him off to school.

In school, he finds himself in a dual world, under two dispensations. There is the world of the boys, where the point of honor is to be untameable, always ready to fight, ruthless in taking the conceit out of anyone who ventures to give himself airs of superior knowledge or taste, and generally to take Lucifer for one's model. And there is the world of the masters, the world of discipline, submission, diligence, obedience, and continual and shameless assumption of moral and intellectual authority. Thus the schoolboy hears both sides, and is so far better off than the homebred boy who hears only one. But the two sides are not fairly presented. They are presented as good and evil, as vice and virtue, as villainy and heroism. The boy feels mean and cowardly when he obeys, and selfish and rascally when he disobeys. He looses his moral courage just as he comes to hate books and languages. In the end, John Ruskin, tied so close to his mother's apron-string that he did not escape even when he went to Oxford, and John Stuart Mill, whose father ought to have been prosecuted for laying his son's childhood waste with lessons, were superior, as products of training, to our schoolboys. They were very conspicuously superior in moral courage; and though they did not distinguish themselves at cricket and football, they had quite as much physical hardihood as any civilized man needs. But it is to be observed that Ruskin's parents were wise people who gave John a full share in their own life, and put up with his presence both at home and abroad when they must sometimes have been very weary of him; and Mill, as it happens, was deliberately educated to challenge all the most sacred institutions of his country. The households they were brought up in were no more average households than a Montessori school is an average school.

The Comings of Age of Children

All this inculcated adult docility, which wrecks every civilization as it is wrecking ours, is inhuman and unnatural. We must reconsider our institution of the Coming of Age, which is too late for some purposes, and too early for others. There should be a series of Coming of Ages for every individual. The mammals have their first coming of age when they are weaned; and it is noteworthy that this rather cruel and selfish operation on the part of the parent has to be performed resolutely, with claws and teeth; for your little mammal does not want to be weaned, and yields only to a pretty rough assertion of the right of the parent to be relieved of the child as soon as the child is old enough to bear the separation. The same thing occurs with children: they hang on to the mother's apron-string and the father's coat tails as long as they can, often baffling those sensitive parents who know that children should think for themselves and fend for themselves, but are too kind to throw them on their own resources with the ferocity of the domestic cat. The child should have its first coming of age when it is weaned, another when it can talk, another when it can walk, another when it can dress itself without assistance; and when it can read, write, count money, and pass an examination in going a simple errand involving a purchase and a journey by rail or other public method of locomotion, it should have quite a majority. At present the children of laborers are soon mobile and able to shift for themselves, whereas it is possible to find grown-up women in the rich classes who are actually afraid to take a walk in the streets unattended and unprotected. It is true that this is a superstition from the time when a retinue was part of the state of persons of quality, and the unattended person was supposed to be a common person of no quality, earning a living; but this has now become so absurd that children and young women are no longer told why they are forbidden to go about alone, and have to be persuaded that the streets are dangerous places, which of course they are; but people who are not educated to live dangerously have only half a life, and are more likely to die miserably after all than those who have taken all the common risks of freedom from their childhood onward as matters of course.

The Conflict of Wills

The world wags in spite of its schools and its families because both schools and families are mostly very largely anarchic: parents and schoolmasters are good-natured or weak or lazy; and children are docile and affectionate and very shortwinded in their fits of naughtiness; and so most families slummock along and muddle through until the children cease to be children. In the few cases when the parties are energetic and determined, the child is crushed or the parent is reduced to a cipher, as the case may be. When the opposed forces are neither of them strong enough to annihilate the other, there is serious trouble: that is how we get those feuds between parent and child which recur to our memory so ironically when we hear people sentimentalizing about natural affection. We even get tragedies; for there is nothing so tragic to contemplate or so devastating to suffer as the oppression of will without conscience; and the whole tendency of our family and school system is to set the will of the parent and the school despot above conscience as something that must be deferred to abjectly and absolutely for its own sake.

The strongest, fiercest force in nature is human will. It is the highest organization we know of the will that has created the whole universe. Now all honest civilization, religion, law, and convention is an attempt to keep this force within beneficent bounds. What corrupts civilization, religion, law, and convention (and they are at present pretty nearly as corrupt as they dare) is the constant attempts made by the wills of individuals and classes to thwart the wills and enslave the powers of other individuals and classes. The powers of the parent and the schoolmaster, and of their public analogues the lawgiver and the judge, become instruments of tyranny in the hands of those who are too narrow-minded to understand law and exercise judgment; and in their hands (with us they mostly fall into such hands) law becomes tyranny. And what is a tyrant? Quite simply a person who says to another person, young or old, "You shall do as I tell you; you shall make what I want; you shall profess my creed; you shall have no will of your own; and your powers shall be at the disposal of my will." It has come to this at last: that the phrase "she has a will of her own," or "he has a will of his own" has come to denote a person of exceptional obstinacy and self-assertion. And even persons of good natural disposition, if brought up to expect such deference, are roused to unreasoning fury, and sometimes to the commission of atrocious crimes, by the slightest challenge to their authority. Thus a laborer may be dirty, drunken, untruthful, slothful, untrustworthy in every way without exhausting the indulgence of the country house. But let him dare to be "disrespectful" and he is a lost man, though he be the cleanest, soberest, most diligent, most veracious, most trustworthy man in the county. Dickens's instinct for detecting social cankers never served him better than when he shewed us Mrs Heep teaching her son to "be umble," knowing that if he carried out that precept he might be pretty well anything else he liked. The maintenance of deference to our wills becomes a mania which will carry the best of us to any extremity.

We will allow a village of Egyptian fellaheen or Indian tribesmen to live the lowest life they please among themselves without molestation; but let one of them slay an Englishman or even strike him on the strongest provocation, and straightway we go stark mad, burning and destroying, shooting and shelling, flogging and hanging, if only such survivors as we may leave are thoroughly cowed in the presence of a man with a white face. In the committee room of a local council or city corporation, the humblest employees of the committee find defenders if they complain of harsh treatment. Gratuities are voted, indulgences and holidays are pleaded for, delinquencies are excused in the most sentimental manner provided only the employee, however patent a hypocrite or incorrigible a slacker, is hat in hand. But let the most obvious measure of justice be demanded by the secretary of a Trade Union in terms which omit all expressions of subservience, and it is with the greatest difficulty that the cooler-headed can defeat angry motions that the letter be thrown into the waste paper basket and the committee proceed to the next business.

The Demagogue's Opportunity

And the employee has in him the same fierce impulse to impose his will without respect for the will of others. Democracy is in practice nothing but a device for cajoling from him the vote he refuses to arbitrary authority. He will not vote for Coriolanus; but when an experienced demagogue comes along and says, "Sir: you are the dictator: the voice of the people is the voice of God; and I am only your very humble servant," he says at once, "All right: tell me what to dictate," and is presently enslaved more effectually with his own silly consent than Coriolanus would ever have enslaved him without asking his leave. And the trick by which the demagogue defeats Coriolanus is played on him in his turn by his inferiors. Everywhere we see the cunning succeeding in the world by seeking a rich or powerful master and practising on his lust for subservience. The political adventurer who gets into parliament by offering himself to the poor voter, not as his representative but as his will-less soulless "delegate," is himself the dupe of a clever wife who repudiates Votes for Women, knowing well that whilst the man is master, the man's mistress will rule. Uriah Heep may be a crawling creature; but his crawling takes him upstairs.

Thus does the selfishness of the will turn on itself, and obtain by flattery what it cannot seize by open force. Democracy becomes the latest trick of tyranny:

"womanliness" becomes the latest wile of prostitution.

Between parent and child the same conflict wages and the same destruction of character ensues. Parents set themselves to bend the will of their children to their own - to break their stubborn spirit, as they call it - with the ruthlessness of Grand Inquisitors. Cunning, unscrupulous children learn all the arts of the sneak in circumventing tyranny: children of better character are cruelly distressed and more or less lamed for life by it.

Our Quarrelsomeness

As between adults, we find a general quarrelsomeness which makes political reform as impossible to most Englishmen as to hogs. Certain sections of the nation get cured of this disability. University men, sailors, and politicians are comparatively free from it, because the communal life of the University, the fact that in a ship a man must either learn to consider others or else go overboard or into irons, and the habit of working on committees and ceasing to expect more of one's own way than is included in the greatest common measure of the committee, educate the will socially. But no one who has ever had to guide a committee of ordinary private Englishmen through their first attempts at collective action, in committee or otherwise, can retain any illusions as to the appalling effects on our national manners and character of the organization of the home and the school as petty tyrannies, and the absence of all teaching of self-respect and training in self-assertion. Bullied and ordered about, the Englishman obeys like a sheep, evades like a knave, or tries to murder his oppressor. Merely criticized or opposed in committee, or invited to consider anybody's views but his own, he feels personally insulted and wants to resign or leave the room unless he is apologized to. And his panic and bewilderment when he sees that the older hands at the work have no patience with him and do not intend to treat him as infallible, are pitiable as far as they are anything but ludicrous. That is what comes of not being taught to consider other people's wills, and left to submit to them or to over-ride them as if they were the winds and the weather. Such a state of mind is incompatible not only with the democratic introduction of high civilization, but with the comprehension and maintenance of such civilized institutions as have been introduced by benevolent and intelligent despots and aristocrats.

We Must Reform Society before we can Reform Ourselves

When we come to the positive problem of what to do with children if we are to give up the established plan, we find the difficulties so great that we begin to understand why so many people who detest the system and look back with loathing on their own schooldays, must helplessly send their children to the very schools they themselves were sent to, because there is no alternative except abandoning the children to undisciplined vagabondism. Man in society must do as everybody else does in his class: only fools and romantic novices imagine that freedom is a mere matter of the readiness of the individual to snap his fingers at convention. It is true that most of us live in a condition of quite unnecessary inhibition, wearing ugly and uncomfortable clothes, making ourselves and other people miserable by the heathen horrors of mourning, staying away from the theatre because we cannot afford the stalls and are ashamed to go to the pit, and in dozens of other ways enslaving ourselves when there are comfortable alternatives open to us without any real drawbacks. The contemplation of these petty slaveries, and of the triumphant ease with which sensible people throw them off, creates an impression that if we only take Johnson's advice to free our minds from cant, we can achieve freedom. But if we all freed our minds from cant we should find that for the most part we should have to go on doing the necessary work of the world exactly as we did it before until we organized new and free methods of doing it. Many people believed in secondary co-education (boys and girls taught together) before schools like Bedales were founded: indeed the practice was common enough in elementary schools and in Scotland; but their belief did not help them until Bedales and St George's were organized; and there are still not nearly enough co-educational schools in existence to accommodate all the children of the parents who believe in co-education up to university age, even if they could always afford the fees of these exceptional schools. It may be edifying to tell a duke that our public schools are all wrong in their constitution and methods, or a costermonger that children should be treated as in Goethe's Wilhelm Meister instead of as they are treated at the elementary school at the corner of his street; but what are the duke and the coster to do? Neither of them has any effective choice in the matter: their children must either go to the schools that are, or to no school at all. And as the duke thinks with reason that his son will be a lout or a milksop or a prig if he does not go to school, and the coster knows that his son will become an illiterate hooligan if he is left to the streets, there is no real alternative for either of them. Child life must be socially organized: no parent, rich or poor, can choose institutions that do not exist; and the private enterprise of individual school masters appealing to a group of well-to-do parents, though it may shew what can be done by enthusiasts with new methods, cannot touch the mass of our children. For the average parent or child nothing is really available except the established practice; and this is what makes it so important that the established practice should be a sound one, and so useless for clever individuals to disparage it unless they can organize an alternative practice and make it, too, general.

The Pursuit of Manners

If you cross-examine the duke and the coster, you will find that they are not concerned for the scholastic attainments of their children. Ask the duke whether he could pass the standard examination of twelve-year-old children in elementary schools, and he will admit, with an entirely placid smile, that he would almost certainly be ignominiously plucked. And he is so little ashamed of or disadvantaged by his condition that he is not prepared to spend an hour in remedying it. The coster may resent the inquiry instead of being amused by it; but his answer, if true, will be the same. What they both want for their children is the communal training, the apprenticeship to society, the lessons in holding one's own among people of all sorts with whom one is not, as in the home, on privileged terms. These can be acquired only by "mixing with the world," no matter how wicked the world is. No parent cares twopence whether his children can write Latin hexameters or repeat the dates of the accession of all the English monarchs since the Conqueror; but all parents are earnestly anxious about the manners of their children. Better Claude Duval than Kaspar Hauser. Laborers who are contemptuously anti-clerical in their opinions will send their daughters to the convent school because the nuns teach them some sort of gentleness of speech and behavior. And peers who tell you that our public schools are rotten through and through, and that our

Universities ought to be razed to the foundations, send their sons to Eton and Oxford, Harrow and Cambridge, not only because there is nothing else to be done, but because these places, though they turn out blackguards and ignoramuses and boobies galore, turn them out with the habits and manners of the society they belong to. Bad as those manners are in many respects, they are better than no manners at all. And no individual or family can possibly teach them. They can be acquired only by living in an organized community in which they are traditional.

Thus we see that there are reasons for the segregation of children even in families where the great reason: namely, that children are nuisances to adults, does not press very hardly, as, for instance, in the houses of the very poor, who can send their children to play in the streets, or the houses of the very rich, which are so large that the children's quarters can be kept out of the parents' way like the servants' quarters.

Not too much Wind on the Heath, Brother

What, then, is to be done? For the present, unfortunately, little except propagating the conception of Children's Rights. Only the achievement of economic equality through Socialism can make it possible to deal thoroughly with the question from the point of view of the total interest of the community, which must always consist of grown-up children. Yet economic equality, like all simple and obvious arrangements, seems impossible to people brought up as children are now. Still, something can be done even within class limits. Large communities of children of the same class are possible today; and voluntary organization of outdoor life for children has already begun in Boy Scouting and excursions of one kind or another. The discovery that anything, even school life, is better for the child than home life, will become an over-ridden hobby; and we shall presently be told by our faddists that anything, even camp life, is better than school life. Some blundering beginnings of this are already perceptible. There is a movement for making our British children into priggish little barefooted vagabonds, all talking like that born fool George Borrow, and supposed to be splendidly healthy because they would die if they slept in rooms with the windows shut, or perhaps even with a roof over their heads. Still, this is a fairly healthy folly; and it may do something to establish Mr Harold Cox's claim of a Right to Roam as the basis of a much needed law compelling proprietors of land to provide plenty of gates in their fences, and to leave them unlocked when there are no growing crops to be damaged nor bulls to be encountered, instead of, as at present, imprisoning the human race in dusty or muddy thoroughfares between walls of barbed wire.

The reaction against vagabondage will come from the children themselves. For them freedom will not mean the expensive kind of savagery now called "the simple life." Their natural disgust with the visions of cockney book fanciers blowing themselves out with "the wind on the heath, brother," and of anarchists who are either too weak to understand that men are strong and free in proportion to the social pressure they can stand and the complexity of the obligations they are prepared to undertake, or too strong to realize that what is freedom to them may be terror and bewilderment to others, will drive them back to the home and the school if these have meanwhile learned the lesson that children are independent human beings and have rights.

Wanted: a Child's Magna Charta

Whether we shall presently be discussing a Juvenile Magna Charta or Declaration of Rights by way of including children in the Constitution is a question on which I leave others to speculate. But if it could once be established that a child has an adult's Right of Egress from uncomfortable places and unpleasant company, and there were children's lawyers to sue pedagogues and others for assault and imprisonment, there would be an amazing change in the behavior of schoolmasters, the quality of school books, and the amenities of school life. That Consciousness of Consent which, even in its present delusive form, has enabled Democracy to oust tyrannical systems in spite of all its vulgarities and stupidities and rancors and ineptitudes and ignorances, would operate as powerfully among children as it does now among grown-ups. No doubt the pedagogue would promptly turn demagogue, and woo his scholars by all the arts of demagogy; but none of these arts can easily be so dishonorable or mischievous as the art of caning. And, after all, if larger liberties are attached to the acquisition of knowledge, and the child finds that it can no more go to the seaside without a knowledge of the multiplication and pence tables than it can be an astronomer without mathematics, it will learn the multiplication table, which is more than it always does at present, in spite of all the canings and keepings in.

The Pursuit of Learning

When the Pursuit of Learning comes to mean the pursuit of learning by the child instead of the pursuit of the child by Learning, cane in hand, the danger will be precocity of the intellect, which is just as undesirable as precocity of the emotions. We still have a silly habit of talking and thinking as if intellect were a mechanical process and not a passion; and in spite of the German tutors who confess openly that three out of every five of the young men they coach for examinations are lamed for life thereby; in spite of Dickens and his picture of little Paul Dombey dying of lessons, we persist in heaping on growing children and adolescent youths and maidens tasks Pythagoras would have declined out of common regard for his own health and common modesty as to his own capacity. And this overwork is not all the effect of compulsion; for the average schoolmaster does not compel his scholars to learn: he only scolds and punishes them if they do not, which is quite a different thing, the net effect being that the school prisoners need not learn unless they like. Nay, it is sometimes remarked that the school dunce - meaning the one who does not like - often turns out well afterwards, as if idleness were a sign of ability and character. A much more sensible explanation is that the so-called dunces are not exhausted before they begin the serious business of life. It is said that boys will be boys; and one can only add one wishes they would. Boys really want to be manly, and are unfortunately encouraged thoughtlessly in this very dangerous and overstraining aspiration. All the people who have really worked (Herbert Spencer for instance) warn us against work as earnestly as some people warn us against drink. When learning is placed on the voluntary footing of sport, the teacher will find himself saying every day "Run away and play: you have worked as much as is good for you." Trying to make children leave school will be like trying to make them go to bed; and it will be necessary to surprise them with the idea that teaching is work, and that the teacher is tired and must go play or rest or eat: possibilities always concealed by that infamous humbug the current schoolmaster, who achieves a spurious divinity and a witch doctor's authority by persuading children that he is nothuman, just as ladies persuade them that they have no legs.

Children and Game: a Proposal

Of the many wild absurdities of our existing social order perhaps the most grotesque is the costly and strictly enforced reservation of large tracts of country as deer forests and breeding grounds for pheasants whilst there is so little provision of the kind made for children. I have more than once thought of trying to introduce the shooting of children as a sport, as the children would then be preserved very carefully for ten months in the year, thereby reducing their death rate far more than the fusillades of the sportsmen during the other two would raise it. At present the killing of a fox except by a pack of foxhounds is regarded with horror; but you may and do kill children in a hundred and fifty ways provided you do not shoot them or set a pack of dogs on them. It must be admitted that the foxes have the best of it; and indeed a glance at our pheasants, our deer, and our children will convince the most sceptical that the children have decidedly the worst of it.

This much hope, however, can be extracted from the present state of things. It is so fantastic, so mad, so apparently impossible, that no scheme of reform need ever henceforth be discredited on the ground that it is fantastic or mad or apparently impossible. It is the sensible schemes, unfortunately, that are hopeless in England. Therefore I have great hopes that my own views, though fundamentally sensible, can be made to appear fantastic enough to have a chance.

First, then, I lay it down as a prime condition of sane society, obvious as such to anyone but an idiot, that in any decent community, children should find in every part of their native country, food, clothing, lodging, instruction, and parental kindness for the asking. For the matter of that, so should adults; but the two cases differ in that as these commodities do not grow on the bushes, the adults cannot have them unless they themselves organize and provide the supply, whereas the children must have them as if by magic, with nothing to do but rub the lamp, like Aladdin, and have their needs satisfied.

The Parents' Intolerable Burden

There is nothing new in this: it is how children have always had and must always have their needs satisfied. The parent has to play the part of Aladdin's djinn; and many a parent has sunk beneath the burden of this service. All the novelty we need is to organize it so that instead of the individual child fastening like a parasite on its own particular parents, the whole body of children should be thrown not only upon the whole body of parents, but upon the celibates and childless as well, whose present exemption from a full share in the social burden of children is obviously unjust and unwholesome. Today it is easy to find a widow who has at great cost to herself in pain, danger, and disablement, borne six or eight children. In the same town you will find rich bachelors and old maids, and married couples with no children or with families voluntarily limited to two or three. The eight children do not belong to the woman in any real or legal sense. When she has reared them they pass away from her into the community as independent persons, marrying strangers, working for strangers, spending on the community the life that has been built up at her expense. No more monstrous injustice could be imagined than that the burden of rearing the children should fall on her alone and not on the celibates and the selfish as well.

This is so far recognized that already the child finds, wherever it goes, a school for it, and somebody to force it into the school; and more and more these schools are being driven by the mere logic of facts to provide the children with meals, with boots, with spectacles, with dentists and doctors. In fact, when the child's parents are destitute or not to be found, bread, lodging, and clothing are provided. It is true that they are provided grudgingly and on conditions infamous enough to draw down abundant fire from Heaven upon us every day in the shape of crime and disease and vice; but still the practice of keeping children barely alive at the charge of the community is established; and there is no need for me to argue about it. I propose only two extensions of the practice. One is to provide for all the child's reasonable human wants, on which point, if you differ from me, I shall take leave to say that you are socially a fool and personally an inhuman wretch. The other is that these wants should be supplied in complete freedom from compulsory schooling or compulsory anything except restraint from crime, though, as they can be supplied only by social organization, the child must be conscious of and subject to the conditions of that organization, which may involve such portions of adult responsibility and duty as a child may be able to bear according to its age, and which will in any case prevent it from forming the vagabond and anarchist habit of mind.

One more exception might be necessary: compulsory freedom. I am sure that a child should not be imprisoned in a school. I am not so sure that it should not sometimes be driven out into the open - imprisoned in the woods and on the mountains, as it were. For there are frowsty children, just as there are frowsty adults, who dont want freedom. This morbid result of over-domestication would, let us hope, soon disappear with its cause.

Mobilization

Those who see no prospect held out to them by this except a country in which all the children shall be roaming savages, should consider, first, whether their condition would be any worse than that of the little caged savages of today, and second, whether either children or adults are so apt to run wild that it is necessary to tether them fast to one neighborhood to prevent a general dissolution of society. My own observation leads me to believe that we are not half mobilized enough. True, I cannot deny that we are more mobile than we were. You will still find in the home counties old men who have never been to London, and who tell you that they once went to Winchester or St Albans much as if they had been to the South Pole; but they are not so common as the clerk who has been to Paris or to Lovely Lucerne, and who "goes away somewhere" when he has a holiday. His grandfather never had a holiday, and, if he had, would no more have dreamed of crossing the Channel than of taking a box at the Opera. But with all allowance for the Polytechnic excursion and the tourist agency, our inertia is still appalling. I confess to having once spent nine years in London without putting my nose outside it; and though this was better, perhaps, than the restless globe-trotting vagabondage of the idle rich, wandering from hotel to hotel and never really living anywhere, yet I should no more have done it if I had been properly mobilized in my childhood than I should have worn the same suit of clothes all that time (which, by the way, I very nearly did, my professional income not having as yet begun to sprout). There are masses of people who could afford at least a trip to Margate, and a good many who could afford a trip round the world, who are more immovable than Aldgate pump. To others, who would move if they knew how, travelling is surrounded with imaginary difficulties and terrors. In short, the difficulty is not to fix people, but to root them up. We keep repeating the silly proverb that a rolling stone gathers no moss, as if moss were a desirable parasite. What we mean is that a vagabond does not prosper. Even this is not true, if prosperity means enjoyment as well as responsibility and money. The real misery of vagabondage is the misery of having nothing to do and nowhere to go, the misery of being derelict of God and Man, the misery of the idle, poor or rich. And this is one of the miseries of unoccupied childhood. The unoccupied adult, thus afflicted, tries many distractions which are, to say the least, unsuited to children. But one of them, the distraction of seeing the world, is innocent and beneficial. Also it is childish, being a continuation of what nurses call "taking notice," by which a child becomes experienced. It is pitiable nowadays to see men and women doing after the age of 45 all the travelling and sightseeing they should have done before they were 15. Mere wondering and staring at things is an important part of a child's education: that is why children can be thoroughly mobilized without making vagabonds of them. A vagabond is at home nowhere because he wanders: a child should wander because it ought to be at home everywhere. And if it has its papers and its passports, and gets what it requires not by begging and pilfering, but from responsible agents of the community as of right, and with some formal acknowledgment of the obligations it is incurring and a knowledge of the fact that these obligations are being recorded: if, further, certain qualifications are exacted before it is promoted from permission to go as far as its legs will carry it to using mechanical aids to locomotion, it can roam without much danger of gypsification.

Under such circumstances the boy or girl could always run away, and never be lost; and on no other conditions can a child be free without being also a homeless outcast.

Parents could also run away from disagreeable children or drive them out of doors or even drop their acquaintance, temporarily or permanently, without inhumanity. Thus both parties would be on their good behavior, and not, as at present, on their filial or parental behavior, which, like all unfree behavior, is mostly bad behavior.

As to what other results might follow, we had better wait and see; for nobody now alive can imagine what customs and institutions would grow up in societies of free children. Child laws and child fashions, child manners and child morals are now not tolerated; but among free children there would certainly be surprising developments in this direction. I do not think there would be any danger of free children behaving as badly as grown-up people do now because they have never been free. They could hardly behave worse, anyhow.

Children's Rights and Parents' Wrongs

A very distinguished man once assured a mother of my acquaintance that she would never know what it meant to be hurt until she was hurt through her children. Children are extremely cruel without intending it; and in ninety-nine cases out of a hundred the reason is that they do not conceive their elders as having any human feelings. Serve the elders right, perhaps, for posing as superhuman! The penalty of the impostor is not that he is found out (he very seldom is) but that he is taken for what he pretends to be, and treated as such. And to be treated as anything but what you really are may seem pleasant to the imagination when the treatment is above your merits; but in actual experience it is often quite the reverse. When I was a very small boy, my romantic imagination, stimulated by early doses of fiction, led me to brag to a still smaller boy so outrageously that he, being a simple soul, really believed me to be an invincible hero. I cannot remember whether this pleased me much; but I do remember very distinctly that one day this admirer of mine, who had a pet goat, found the animal in the hands of a larger boy than either of us, who mocked him and refused to restore the animal to his rightful owner. Whereupon, naturally, he came weeping to me, and demanded that I should rescue the goat and annihilate the aggressor. My terror was beyond description: fortunately for me, it imparted such a ghastliness to my voice and aspect as I under the eye of my poor little dupe, advanced on the enemy with that hideous extremity of cowardice which is called the courage of despair, and said "You let go that goat," that he abandoned his prey and fled, to my unforgettable, unspeakable relief. I have never since exaggerated my prowess in bodily combat.

Now what happened to me in the adventure of the goat happens very often to parents, and would happen to schoolmasters if the prison door of the school did not shut out the trials of life. I remember once, at school, the resident head master was brought down to earth by the sudden illness of his wife. In the confusion that ensued it became necessary to leave one of the schoolrooms without a master. I was in the class that occupied that schoolroom. To have sent us home would have been to break the fundamental bargain with our parents by which the school was bound to keep us out of their way for half the day at all hazards. Therefore an appeal had to be made to our better feelings: that is, to our common humanity, not to make a noise. But the head master had never admitted any common humanity with us. We had been carefully broken in to regard him as a being quite aloof from and above us: one not subject to error or suffering or death or illness or mortality. Consequently sympathy was impossible; and if the unfortunate lady did not perish, it was because, as I now comfort myself with guessing, she was too much pre-occupied with her own pains, and possibly making too much noise herself, to be conscious of the pandemonium downstairs.

A great deal of the fiendishness of schoolboys and the cruelty of children to their elders is produced just in this way. Elders cannot be superhuman beings and suffering fellow-creatures at the same time. If you pose as a little god, you must pose for better for worse.

How Little We Know About Our Parents

The relation between parent and child has cruel moments for the parent even when money is no object, and the material worries are delegated to servants and school teachers. The child and the parent are strangers to one another necessarily, because their ages must differ widely. Read Goethe's autobiography; and note that though he was happy in his parents and had exceptional powers of observation, divination, and story-telling, he knew less about his father and mother than about most of the other people he mentions. I myself was never on bad terms with my mother: we lived together until I was forty-two years old, absolutely without the smallest friction of any kind; yet when her death set me thinking curiously about our relations, I realized that I knew very little about her. Introduce me to a strange woman who was a child when I was a child, a girl when I was a boy, an adolescent when I was an adolescent; and if we take naturally to one another I will know more of her and she of me at the end of forty days (I had almost said of forty minutes) than I knew of my mother at the end of forty years. A contemporary stranger is a novelty and an enigma, also a possibility; but a mother is like a broomstick or like the sun in the heavens, it does not matter which as far as one's knowledge of her is concerned: the broomstick is there and the sun is there; and whether the child is beaten by it or warmed and enlightened by it, it accepts it as a fact in nature, and does not conceive it as having had youth, passions, and weaknesses, or as still growing, yearning, suffering, and learning. If I meet a widow I may ask her all about her marriage; but what son ever dreams of asking his mother about her marriage, or could endure to hear of it without violently breaking off the old sacred relationship between them, and ceasing to be her child or anything more to her than the first man in the street might be?

Yet though in this sense the child cannot realize its parent's humanity, the parent can realize the child's; for the parents with their experience of life have none of the illusions about the child that the child has about the parents; and the consequence is that the child can hurt its parents' feelings much more than its parents can hurt the child's, because the child, even when there has been none of the deliberate hypocrisy by which children are taken advantage of by their elders, cannot conceive the parent as a fellow-creature, whilst the parents know very well that the children are only themselves over again. The child cannot conceive that its blame or contempt or want of interest could possibly hurt its parent, and therefore expresses them all with an indifference which has given rise to the term enfant terrible (a tragic term in spite of the jests connected with it); whilst the parent can suffer from such slights and reproaches more from a child than from anyone else, even when the child is not beloved, because the child is so unmistakably sincere in them.

Our Abandoned Mothers

Take a very common instance of this agonizing incompatibility. A widow brings up her son to manhood. He meets a strange woman, and goes off with and marries her, leaving his mother desolate. It does not occur to him that this is at all hard on her: he does it as a matter of course, and actually expects his mother to receive, on terms of special affection, the woman for whom she has been abandoned. If he shewed any sense of what he was doing, any remorse; if he mingled his tears with hers and asked her not to think too hardly of him because he had obeyed the inevitable destiny of a man to leave his father and mother and cleave to his wife, she could give him her blessing and accept her bereavement with dignity and without reproach. But the man never dreams of such considerations. To him his mother's feeling in the matter, when she betrays it, is unreasonable, ridiculous, and even odious, as shewing a prejudice against his adorable bride.

I have taken the widow as an extreme and obvious case; but there are many husbands and wives who are tired of their consorts, or disappointed in them, or estranged from them by infidelities; and these parents, in losing a son or a daughter through marriage, may be losing everything they care for. No parent's love is as innocent as the love of a child: the exclusion of all conscious sexual feeling from it does not exclude the bitterness, jealousy, and despair at loss which characterize sexual passion: in fact, what is called a pure love may easily be more selfish and jealous than a carnal one. Anyhow, it is plain matter of fact that naively selfish people sometimes try with fierce jealousy to prevent their children marrying.

Family Affection

Until the family as we know it ceases to exist, nobody will dare to analyze parental affection as distinguished from that general human sympathy which has secured to many an orphan fonder care in a stranger's house than it would have received from its actual parents. Not even Tolstoy, in The Kreutzer Sonata, has said all that we suspect about it. When it persists beyond the period at which it ceases to be necessary to the child's welfare, it is apt to be morbid; and we are probably wrong to inculcate its deliberate cultivation. The natural course is for the parents and children to cast off the specific parental and filial relation when they are no longer necessary to one another. The child does this readily enough to form fresh ties, closer and more fascinating. Parents are not always excluded from such compensations: it happens sometimes that when the children go out at the door the lover comes in at the window. Indeed it happens now oftener than it used to, because people remain much longer in the sexual arena. The cultivated Jewess no longer cuts off her hair at her marriage. The British matron has discarded her cap and her conscientious ugliness; and a bishop's wife at fifty has more of the air of a femme galante than an actress had at thirty-five in her grandmother's time. But as people marry later, the facts of age and time still inexorably condemn most parents to comparative solitude when their children marry. This may be a privation and may be a relief: probably in healthy circumstances it is no worse than a salutary change of habit; but even at that it is, for the moment at least, a wrench. For though parents and children sometimes dislike one another, there is an experience of succor and a habit of dependence and expectation formed in infancy which naturally attaches a child to its parent or to its nurse (a foster parent) in a quite peculiar way. A benefit to the child may be a burden to the parent; but people become attached to their burdens sometimes more than the burdens are attached to them; and to "suffer little children" has become an affectionate impulse deep in our nature.

Now there is no such impulse to suffer our sisters and brothers, our aunts and uncles, much less our cousins. If we could choose our relatives, we might, by selecting congenial ones, mitigate the repulsive effect of the obligation to like them and to admit them to our intimacy. But to have a person imposed on us as a brother merely because he happens to have the same parents is unbearable when, as may easily happen, he is the sort of person we should carefully avoid if he were anyone else's brother. All Europe (except Scotland, which has clans instead of families) draws the line at second cousins. Protestantism draws it still closer by making the first cousin a marriageable stranger; and the only reason for not drawing it at sisters and brothers is that the institution of the family compels us to spend our childhood with them, and thus imposes on us a curious relation in which familiarity destroys romantic charm, and is yet expected to create a specially warm affection. Such a relation is dangerously factitious and unnatural; and the practical moral is that the less said at home about specific family affection the better. Children, like grown-up people, get on well enough together if they are not pushed down one another's throats; and grown-up relatives will get on together in proportion to their separation and their care not to presume on their blood relationship. We should let children's feelings take their natural course without prompting. I have seen a child scolded and called unfeeling because it did not occur to it to make a theatrical demonstration of affectionate delight when its mother returned after an absence: a typical example of the way in which spurious family sentiment is stoked up. We are, after all, sociable animals; and if we are let alone in the matter of our affections, and well brought up otherwise, we shall not get on any the worse with particular people because they happen to be our brothers and sisters and cousins. The danger lies in assuming that we shall get on any better.

The main point to grasp here is that families are not kept together at present by family feeling but by human feeling. The family cultivates sympathy and mutual help and consolation as any other form of kindly association cultivates them; but the addition of a dictated compulsory affection as an attribute of near kinship is not only unnecessary, but positively detrimental; and the alleged tendency of modern social development to break up the family need alarm nobody. We cannot break up the facts of kinship nor eradicate its natural emotional consequences. What we can do and ought to do is to set people free to behave naturally and to change their behavior as circumstances change. To impose on a citizen of London the family duties of a Highland cateran in the eighteenth century is as absurd as to compel him to carry a claymore and target instead of an umbrella. The civilized man has no special use for cousins; and he may presently find that he has no special use for brothers and sisters. The parent seems likely to remain indispensable; but there is no reason why that natural tie should be made the excuse for unnatural aggravations of it, as crushing to the parent as they are oppressive to the child. The mother and father will not always have to shoulder the burthen of maintenance which should fall on the Atlas shoulders of the fatherland and motherland. Pending such reforms and emancipations, a shattering break-up of the parental home must remain one of the normal incidents of marriage. The parent is left lonely and the child is not. Woe to the old if they have no impersonal interests, no convictions, no public causes to advance, no tastes or hobbies! It is well to be a mother but not to be a mother-in-law; and if men were cut off artificially from intellectual and public interests as women are, the father-in-law would be as deplorable a figure in popular tradition as the mother-in-law.

It is not to be wondered at that some people hold that blood relationship should be kept a secret from the persons related, and that the happiest condition in this respect is that of the foundling who, if he ever meets his parents or brothers or sisters, passes them by without knowing them. And for such a view there is this to be said: that our family system does unquestionably take the natural bond between members of the same family, which, like all natural bonds, is not too tight to be borne, and superimposes on it a painful burden of forced, inculcated, suggested, and altogether unnecessary affection and responsibility which we should do well to get rid of by making relatives as independent of one another as possible.

The Fate of the Family

The difficulty of inducing people to talk sensibly about the family is the same as that which I pointed out in a previous volume as confusing discussions of marriage. Marriage is not a single invariable institution: it changes from civilization to civilization, from religion to religion, from civil code to civil code, from frontier to frontier. The family is still more variable, because the number of persons constituting a family, unlike the number of persons constituting a marriage, varies from one to twenty: indeed, when a widower with a family marries a widow with a family, and the two produce a third family, even that very high number may be surpassed. And the conditions may vary between opposite extremes: for example, in a London or Paris slum every child adds to the burden of poverty and helps to starve the parents and all the other children, whereas in a settlement of pioneer colonists every child, from the moment it is big enough to lend a hand to the family industry, is an investment in which the only danger is that of temporary over-capitalization. Then there are the variations in family sentiment. Sometimes the family organization is as frankly political as the organization of an army or an industry: fathers being no more expected to be sentimental about their children than colonels about soldiers, or factory owners about their employees, though the mother may be allowed a little tenderness if her character is weak.

The Roman father was a despot: the Chinese father is an object of worship: the sentimental modern western father is often a play-fellow looked to for toys and pocket-money. The farmer sees his children constantly: the squire sees them only during the holidays, and not then oftener than he can help: the tram conductor, when employed by a joint stock company, sometimes never sees them at all.

Under such circumstances phrases like The Influence of Home Life, The Family, The Domestic Hearth, and so on, are no more specific than The Mammals, or The Man In The Street; and the pious generalizations founded so glibly on them by our sentimental moralists are unworkable. When households average twelve persons with the sexes about equally represented, the results may be fairly good. When they average three the results may be very bad indeed; and to lump the two together under the general term The Family is to confuse the question hopelessly. The modern small family is much too stuffy: children "brought up at home" in it are unfit for society. But here again circumstances differ. If the parents live in what is called a garden suburb, where there is a good deal of social intercourse, and the family, instead of keeping itself to itself, as the evil old saying is, and glowering at the neighbors over the blinds of the long street in which nobody knows his neighbor and everyone wishes to deceive him as to his income and social importance, is in effect broken up by school life, by out-of-door habits, and by frank neighborly intercourse through dances and concerts and theatricals and excursions and the like, families of four may turn out much less barbarous citizens than families of ten which attain the Boer ideal of being out of sight of one another's chimney smoke.

All one can say is, roughly, that the homelier the home, and the more familiar the family, the worse for everybody concerned. The family ideal is a humbug and a nuisance: one might as reasonably talk of the barrack ideal, or the forecastle ideal, or any other substitution of the machinery of social organization for the end of it, which must always be the fullest and most capable life: in short, the most godly life. And this significant word reminds us that though the popular conception of heaven includes a Holy Family, it does not attach to that family the notion of a separate home, or a private nursery or kitchen or mother-in-law, or anything that constitutes the family as we know it. Even blood relationship is miraculously abstracted from it; and the Father is the father of all children, the mother the mother of all mothers and babies, and the Son the Son of Man and the Savior of his brothers: one whose chief utterance on the subject of the conventional family was an invitation to all of us to leave our families and follow him, and to leave the dead to bury the dead, and not debauch ourselves at that gloomy festival the family funeral, with its sequel of hideous mourning and grief which is either affected or morbid.

Family Mourning

I do not know how far this detestable custom of mourning is carried in France; but judging from the appearance of the French people I should say that a Frenchwoman goes into mourning for her cousins to the seventeenth degree. The result is that when I cross the Channel I seem to have reached a country devastated by war or pestilence. It is really suffering only from the family. Will anyone pretend that England has not the best of this striking difference? Yet it is such senseless and unnatural conventions as this that make us so impatient of what we call family feeling. Even apart from its insufferable pretensions, the family needs hearty discrediting; for there is hardly any vulnerable part of it that could not be amputated with advantage.

Art Teaching

By art teaching I hasten to say that I do not mean giving children lessons in freehand drawing and perspective. I am simply calling attention to the fact that fine art is the only teacher except torture. I have already pointed out that nobody, except under threat of torture, can read a school book. The reason is that a school book is not a work of art. Similarly, you cannot listen to a lesson or a sermon unless the teacher or the preacher is an artist. You cannot read the Bible if you have no sense of literary art. The reason why the continental European is, to the Englishman or American, so surprisingly ignorant of the Bible, is that the authorized English version is a great work of literary art, and the continental versions are comparatively artless. To read a dull book; to listen to a tedious play or prosy sermon or lecture; to stare at uninteresting pictures or ugly buildings: nothing, short of disease, is more dreadful than this. The violence done to our souls by it leaves injuries and produces subtle maladies which have never been properly studied by psycho-pathologists. Yet we are so inured to it in school, where practically all the teachers are bores trying to do the work of artists, and all the books artless, that we acquire a truly frightful power of enduring boredom. We even acquire the notion that fine art is lascivious and destructive to the character. In church, in the House of Commons, at public meetings, we sit solemnly listening to bores and twaddlers because from the time we could walk or speak we have been snubbed, scolded, bullied, beaten and imprisoned whenever we dared to resent being bored or twaddled at, or to express our natural impatience and derision of bores and twaddlers. And when a man arises with a soul of sufficient native strength to break the bonds of this inculcated reverence and to expose and deride and tweak the noses of our humbugs and panjandrums, like Voltaire or Dickens, we are shocked and scandalized, even when we cannot help laughing. Worse, we dread and persecute those who can see and declare the truth, because their sincerity and insight reflects on our delusion and blindness. We are all like Nell Gwynne's footman, who defended Nell's reputation with his fists, not because he believed her to be what he called an honest woman, but because he objected to be scorned as the footman of one who was no better than she should be.

This wretched power of allowing ourselves to be bored may seem to give the fine arts a chance sometimes. People will sit through a performance of Beethoven's ninth symphony or of Wagner's Ring just as they will sit through a dull sermon or a front bench politician saying nothing for two hours whilst his unfortunate country is perishing through the delay of its business in Parliament. But their endurance is very bad for the ninth symphony, because they never hiss when it is murdered. I have heard an Italian conductor (no longer living) take the adagio of that symphony at a lively allegretto, slowing down for the warmer major sections into the speed and manner of the heroine's death song in a Verdi opera; and the listeners, far from relieving my excruciation by rising with yells of fury and hurling their programs and opera glasses at the miscreant, behaved just as they do when Richter conducts it. The mass of imposture that thrives on this combination of ignorance with despairing endurance is incalculable. Given a public trained from childhood to stand anything tedious, and so saturated with school discipline that even with the doors open and no schoolmasters to stop them they will sit there helplessly until the end of the concert or opera gives them leave to go home; and you will have in great capitals hundreds of thousands of pounds spent every night in the season on professedly artistic entertainments which have no other effect on fine art than to exacerbate the hatred in which it is already secretly held in England.

Fortunately, there are arts that cannot be cut off from the people by bad performances. We can read books for ourselves; and we can play a good deal of fine music for ourselves with the help of a pianola. Nothing stands between us and the actual handwork of the great masters of painting except distance; and modern photographic methods of reproduction are in some cases quite and in many nearly as effective in conveying the artist's message as a modern edition of Shakespear's plays is in conveying the message that first existed in his handwriting. The reproduction of great feats of musical execution is already on the way: the phonograph, for all its wheezing and snarling and braying, is steadily improving in its manners; and what with this improvement on the one hand, and on the other that blessed selective faculty which enables us to ignore a good deal of disagreeable noise if there is a thread of music in the middle of it (few critics of the phonograph seem to be conscious of the very considerable mechanical noise set up by choirs and orchestras) we have at last reached a point at which, for example, a person living in an English village where the church music is the only music, and that music is made by a few well-intentioned ladies with the help of a harmonium, can hear masses by Palestrina very passably executed, and can thereby be led to the discovery that Jackson in F and Hymns Ancient and Modern are not perhaps the last word of beauty and propriety in the praise of God.

In short, there is a vast body of art now within the reach of everybody. The difficulty is that this art, which alone can educate us in grace of body and soul, and which alone can make the history of the past live for us or the hope of the future shine for us, which alone can give delicacy and nobility to our crude lusts, which is the appointed vehicle of inspiration and the method of the communion of saints, is actually branded as sinful among us because, wherever it arises, there is resistance to tyranny, breaking of fetters, and the breath of freedom. The attempt to suppress art is not wholly successful: we might as well try to suppress oxygen. But it is carried far enough to inflict on huge numbers of people a most injurious art starvation, and to corrupt a great deal of the art that is tolerated. You will find in England plenty of rich families with little more culture than their dogs and horses. And you will find poor families, cut off by poverty and town life from the contemplation of the beauty of the earth, with its dresses of leaves, its scarves of cloud, and its contours of hill and valley, who would positively be happier as hogs, so little have they cultivated their humanity by the only effective instrument of culture: art. The dearth is artificially maintained even when there are the means of satisfying it. Story books are forbidden, picture post cards are forbidden, theatres are forbidden, operas are forbidden, circuses are forbidden, sweetmeats are forbidden, pretty colors are forbidden, all exactly as vice is forbidden. The Creator is explicitly prayed to, and implicitly convicted of indecency every day. An association of vice and sin with everything that is delightful and of goodness with everything that is wretched and detestable is set up. All the most perilous (and glorious) appetites and propensities are at once inflamed by starvation and uneducated by art. All the wholesome conditions which art imposes on appetite are waived: instead of cultivated men and women restrained by a thousand delicacies, repelled by ugliness, chilled by vulgarity, horrified by coarseness, deeply and sweetly moved by the graces that art has revealed to them and nursed in them, we get indiscrimmate rapacity in pursuit of pleasure and a parade of the grossest stimulations in catering for it. We have a continual clamor for goodness, beauty, virtue, and sanctity, with such an appalling inability to recognize it or love it when it arrives that it is more dangerous to be a great prophet or poet than to promote twenty companies for swindling simple folk out of their savings. Do not for a moment suppose that uncultivated people are merely indifferent to high and noble qualities. They hate them malignantly. At best, such qualities are like rare and beautiful birds: when they appear the whole country takes down its guns; but the birds receive the statuary tribute of having their corpses stuffed.

And it really all comes from the habit of preventing children from being troublesome. You are so careful of your boy's morals, knowing how troublesome they may be, that you keep him away from the Venus of Milo only to find him in the arms of the scullery maid or someone much worse. You decide that the Hermes of Praxiteles and Wagner's Tristan are not suited for young girls; and your daughter marries somebody appallingly unlike either Hermes or Tristan solely to escape from your parental protection. You have not stifled a single passion nor averted a single danger: you have depraved the passions by starving them, and broken down all the defences which so effectively protect children brought up in freedom. You have men who imagine themselves to be ministers of religion openly declaring that when they pass through the streets they have to keep out in the wheeled traffic to avoid the temptations of the pavement. You have them organizing hunts of the women who tempt them - poor creatures whom no artist would touch without a shudder - and wildly clamoring for more clothes to disguise and conceal the body, and for the abolition of pictures, statues, theatres, and pretty colors. And incredible as it seems, these unhappy lunatics are left at large, unrebuked, even admired and revered, whilst artists have to struggle for toleration. To them an undraped human body is the most monstrous, the most blighting, the most obscene, the most unbearable spectacle in the universe. To an artist it is, at its best, the most admirable spectacle in nature, and, at its average, an object of indifference. If every rag of clothing miraculously dropped from the inhabitants of London at noon tomorrow (say as a preliminary to the Great Judgment), the artistic people would not turn a hair; but the artless people would go mad and call on the mountains to hide them. I submit that this indicates a thoroughly healthy state on the part of the artists, and a thoroughly morbid one on the part of the artless. And the healthy state is attainable in a cold country like ours only by familiarity with the undraped figure acquired through pictures, statues, and theatrical representations in which an illusion of natural clotheslessness is produced and made poetic.

In short, we all grow up stupid and mad to just the extent to which we have not been artistically educated; and the fact that this taint of stupidity and madness has to be tolerated because it is general, and is even boasted of as characteristically English, makes the situation all the worse. It is becoming exceedingly grave at present, because the last ray of art is being cut off from our schools by the discontinuance of religious education.

The Impossibility of Secular Education

Now children must be taught some sort of religion. Secular education is an impossibility. Secular education comes to this: that the only reason for ceasing to do evil and learning to do well is that if you do not you will be caned. This is worse than being taught in a church school that if you become a dissenter you will go to hell; for hell is presented as the instrument of something eternal, divine, and inevitable: you cannot evade it the moment the schoolmaster's back is turned. What confuses this issue and leads even highly intelligent religious persons to advocate secular education as a means of rescuing children from the strife of rival proselytizers is the failure to distinguish between the child's personal subjective need for a religion and its right to an impartially communicated historical objective knowledge of all the creeds and Churches. Just as a child, no matter what its race and color may be, should know that there are black men and brown men and yellow men, and, no matter what its political convictions may be, that there are Monarchists and Republicans and Positivists, Socialists and Unsocialists, so it should know that there are Christians and Mahometans and Buddhists and Shintoists and so forth, and that they are on the average just as honest and well-behaved as its own father. For example, it should not be told that Allah is a false god set up by the Turks and Arabs, who will all be damned for taking that liberty; but it should be told that many English people think so, and that many Turks and Arabs think the converse about English people. It should be taught that Allah is simply the name by which God is known to Turks and Arabs, who are just as eligible for salvation as any Christian. Further, that the practical reason why a Turkish child should pray in a mosque and an English child in a church is that as worship is organized in Turkey in mosques in the name of Mahomet and in England in churches in the name of Christ, a Turkish child joining the Church of England or an English child following Mahomet will find that it has no place for its worship and no organization of its religion within its reach. Any other teaching of the history and present facts of religion is false teaching, and is politically extremely dangerous in an empire in which a huge majority of the fellow subjects of the governing island do not profess the religion of that island.

But this objectivity, though intellectually honest, tells the child only what other people believe. What it should itself believe is quite another matter. The sort of Rationalism which says to a child "You must suspend your judgment until you are old enough to choose your religion" is Rationalism gone mad. The child must have a conscience and a code of honor (which is the essence of religion) even if it be only a provisional one, to be revised at its confirmation. For confirmation is meant to signalize a spiritual coming of age, and may be a repudiation. Really active souls have many confirmations and repudiations as their life deepens and their knowledge widens. But what is to guide the child before its first confirmation? Not mere orders, because orders must have a sanction of some sort or why should the child obey them? If, as a Secularist, you refuse to teach any sanction, you must say "You will be punished if you disobey." "Yes," says the child to itself, "if I am found out; but wait until your back is turned and I will do as I like, and lie about it." There can be no objective punishment for successful fraud; and as no espionage can cover the whole range of a child's conduct, the upshot is that the child becomes a liar and schemer with an atrophied conscience. And a good many of the orders given to it are not obeyed after all. Thus the Secularist who is not a fool is forced to appeal to the child's vital impulse towards perfection, to the divine spark; and no resolution not to call this impulse an impulse of loyalty to the Fellowship of the Holy Ghost, or obedience to the Will of God, or any other standard theological term, can alter the fact that the Secularist has stepped outside Secularism and is educating the child religiously, even if he insists on repudiating that pious adverb and substituting the word metaphysically.

Natural Selection as a Religion

We must make up our minds to it therefore that whatever measures we may be forced to take to prevent the recruiting sergeants of the Churches, free or established, from obtaining an exclusive right of entry to schools, we shall not be able to exclude religion from them. The most horrible of all religions: that which teaches us to regard ourselves as the helpless prey of a series of senseless accidents called Natural Selection, is allowed and even welcomed in so-called secular schools because it is, in a sense, the negation of all religion; but for school purposes a religion is a belief which affects conduct; and no belief affects conduct more radically and often so disastrously as the belief that the universe is a product of Natural Selection. What is more, the theory of Natural Selection cannot be kept out of schools, because many of the natural facts that present the most plausible appearance of design can be accounted for by Natural Selection; and it would be so absurd to keep a child in delusive ignorance of so potent a factor in evolution as to keep it in ignorance of radiation or capillary attraction. Even if you make a religion of Natural Selection, and teach the child to regard itself as the irresponsible prey of its circumstances and appetites (or its heredity as you will perhaps call them), you will none the less find that its appetites are stimulated by your encouragement and daunted by your discouragement; that one of its appetites is an appetite for perfection; that if you discourage this appetite and encourage the cruder acquisitive appetites the child will steal and lie and be a nuisance to you; and that if you encourage its appetite for perfection and teach it to attach a peculiar sacredness to it and place it before the other appetites, it will be a much nicer child and you will have a much easier job, at which point you will, in spite of your pseudoscientific jargon, find yourself back in the old-fashioned religious teaching as deep as Dr. Watts and in fact fathoms deeper.

Moral Instruction Leagues

And now the voices of our Moral Instruction Leagues will be lifted, asking whether there is any reason why the appetite for perfection should not be cultivated in rationally scientific terms instead of being associated with the story of Jonah and the great fish and the thousand other tales that grow up round religions. Yes: there are many reasons; and one of them is that children all like the story of Jonah and the whale (they insist on its being a whale in spite of demonstrations by Bible smashers without any sense of humor that Jonah would not have fitted into a whale's gullet - as if the story would be credible of a whale with an enlarged throat) and that no child on earth can stand moral instruction books or catechisms or any other statement of the case for religion in abstract terms. The object of a moral instruction book is not to be rational, scientific, exact, proof against controversy, nor even credible: its object is to make children good; and if it makes them sick instead its place is the waste-paper basket.

Take for an illustration the story of Elisha and the bears. To the authors of the moral instruction books it is in the last degree reprehensible. It is obviously not true as a record of fact; and the picture it gives us of the temper of God (which is what interests an adult reader) is shocking and blasphemous. But it is a capital story for a child. It interests a child because it is about bears; and it leaves the child with an impression that children who poke fun at old gentlemen and make rude remarks about bald heads are not nice children, which is a highly desirable impression, and just as much as a child is capable of receiving from the story. When a story is about God and a child, children take God for granted and criticize the child. Adults do the opposite, and are thereby led to talk great nonsense about the bad effect of Bible stories on infants.

But let no one think that a child or anyone else can learn religion from a teacher or a book or by any academic process whatever. It is only by an unfettered access to the whole body of Fine Art: that is, to the whole body of inspired revelation, that we can build up that conception of divinity to which all virtue is an aspiration. And to hope to find this body of art purified from all that is obsolete or dangerous or fierce or lusty, or to pick and choose what will be good for any particular child, much less for all children, is the shallowest of vanities. Such schoolmasterly selection is neither possible nor desirable. Ignorance of evil is not virtue but imbecility: admiring it is like giving a prize for honesty to a man who has not stolen your watch because he did not know you had one. Virtue chooses good from evil; and without knowledge there can be no choice. And even this is a dangerous simplification of what actually occurs. We are not choosing: we are growing. Were you to cut all of what you call the evil out of a child, it would drop dead. If you try to stretch it to full human stature when it is ten years old, you will simply pull it into two pieces and be hanged. And when you try to do this morally, which is what parents and schoolmasters are doing every day, you ought to be hanged; and some day, when we take a sensible view of the matter, you will be; and serve you right. The child does not stand between a good and a bad angel: what it has to deal with is a middling angel who, in normal healthy cases, wants to be a good angel as fast as it can without killing itself in the process, which is a dangerous one.

Therefore there is no question of providing the child with a carefully regulated access to good art. There is no good art, any more than there is good anything else in the absolute sense. Art that is too good for the child will either teach it nothing or drive it mad, as the Bible has driven many people mad who might have kept their sanity had they been allowed to read much lower forms of literature. The practical moral is that we must read whatever stories, see whatever pictures, hear whatever songs and symphonies, go to whatever plays we like. We shall not like those which have nothing to say to us; and though everyone has a right to bias our choice, no one has a right to deprive us of it by keeping us from any work of art or any work of art from us.

I may now say without danger of being misunderstood that the popular English compromise called Cowper Templeism (unsectarian Bible education) is not so silly as it looks. It is true that the Bible inculcates half a dozen religions: some of them barbarous; some cynical and pessimistic; some amoristic and romantic; some sceptical and challenging; some kindly, simple, and intuitional; some sophistical and intellectual; none suited to the character and conditions of western civilization unless it be the Christianity which was finally suppressed by the Crucifixion, and has never been put into practice by any State before or since. But the Bible contains the ancient literature of a very remarkable Oriental race; and the imposition of this literature, on whatever false pretences, on our children left them more literate than if they knew no literature at all, which was the practical alternative. And as our Authorized Version is a great work of art as well, to know it was better than knowing no art, which also was the practical alternative. It is at least not a school book; and it is not a bad story book, horrible as some of the stories are. Therefore as between the Bible and the blank represented by secular education, the choice is with the Bible.

The Bible

But the Bible is not sufficient. The real Bible of modern Europe is the whole body of great literature in which the inspiration and revelation of Hebrew Scripture has been continued to the present day. Nietzsche's Thus Spake Zoroaster is less comforting to the ill and unhappy than the Psalms; but it is much truer, subtler, and more edifying. The pleasure we get from the rhetoric of the book of Job and its tragic picture of a bewildered soul cannot disguise the ignoble irrelevance of the retort of God with which it closes, or supply the need of such modern revelations as Shelley's Prometheus or The Niblung's Ring of Richard Wagner. There is nothing in the Bible greater in inspiration than Beethoven's ninth symphony; and the power of modern music to convey that inspiration to a modern man is far greater than that of Elizabethan English, which is, except for people steeped in the Bible from childhood like Sir Walter Scott and Ruskin, a dead language.

Besides, many who have no ear for literature or for music are accessible to architecture, to pictures, to statues, to dresses, and to the arts of the stage. Every device of art should be brought to bear on the young; so that they may discover some form of it that delights them naturally; for there will come to all of them that period between dawning adolescence and full maturity when the pleasures and emotions of art will have to satisfy cravings which, if starved or insulted, may become morbid and seek disgraceful satisfactions, and, if prematurely gratified otherwise than poetically, may destroy the stamina of the race. And it must be borne in mind that the most dangerous art for this necessary purpose is the art that presents itself as religious ecstasy. Young people are ripe for love long before they are ripe for religion. Only a very foolish person would substitute the Imitation of Christ for Treasure Island as a present for a boy or girl, or for Byron's Don Juan as a present for a swain or lass. Pickwick is the safest saint for us in our nonage. Flaubert's Temptation of St Anthony is an excellent book for a man of fifty, perhaps the best within reach as a healthy study of visionary ecstasy; but for the purposes of a boy of fifteen Ivanhoe and the Templar make a much better saint and devil. And the boy of fifteen will find this out for himself if he is allowed to wander in a well-stocked literary garden, and hear bands and see pictures and spend his pennies on cinematograph shows. His choice may often be rather disgusting to his elders when they want him to choose the best before he is ready for it. The greatest Protestant Manifesto ever written, as far as I know, is Houston Chamberlain's Foundations of the Nineteenth Century: everybody capable of it should read it. Probably the History of Maria Monk is at the opposite extreme of merit (this is a guess: I have never read it); but it is certain that a boy let loose in a library would go for Maria Monk and have no use whatever for Mr Chamberlain. I should probably have read Maria Monk myself if I had not had the Arabian Nights and their like to occupy me better. In art, children, like adults, will find their level if they are left free to find it, and not restricted to what adults think good for them. Just at present our young people are going mad over ragtimes, apparently because syncopated rhythms are new to them. If they had learnt what can be done with syncopation from Beethoven's third Leonora overture, they would enjoy the ragtimes all the more; but they would put them in their proper place as amusing vulgarities.

Artist Idolatry

But there are more dangerous influences than ragtimes waiting for people brought up in ignorance of fine art. Nothing is more pitiably ridiculous than the wild worship of artists by those who have never been seasoned in youth to the enchantments of art. Tenors and prima donnas, pianists and violinists, actors and actresses enjoy powers of seduction which in the middle ages would have exposed them to the risk of being burnt for sorcery. But as they exercise this power by singing, playing, and acting, no great harm is done except perhaps to themselves. Far graver are the powers enjoyed by brilliant persons who are also connoisseurs in art. The influence they can exercise on young people who have been brought up in the darkness and wretchedness of a home without art, and in whom a natural bent towards art has always been baffled and snubbed, is incredible to those who have not witnessed and understood it. He (or she) who reveals the world of art to them opens heaven to them. They become satellites, disciples, worshippers of the apostle. Now the apostle may be a voluptuary without much conscience. Nature may have given him enough virtue to suffice in a reasonable environment. But this allowance may not be enough to defend him against the temptation and demoralization of finding himself a little god on the strength of what ought to be a quite ordinary culture. He may find adorers in all directions in our uncultivated society among people of stronger character than himself, not one of whom, if they had been artistically educated, would have had anything to learn from him or regarded him as in any way extraordinary apart from his actual achievements as an artist. Tartuffe is not always a priest. Indeed he is not always a rascal: he is often a weak man absurdly credited with omniscience and perfection, and taking unfair advantages only because they are offered to him and he is too weak to refuse. Give everyone his culture, and no one will offer him more than his due.

In thus delivering our children from the idolatry of the artist, we shall not destroy for them the enchantment of art: on the contrary, we shall teach them to demand art everywhere as a condition attainable by cultivating the body, mind, and heart. Art, said Morris, is the expression of pleasure in work. And certainly, when work is made detestable by slavery, there is no art. It is only when learning is made a slavery by tyrannical teachers that art becomes loathsome to the pupil.

"The Machine"

When we set to work at a Constitution to secure freedom for children, we had better bear in mind that the children may not be at all obliged to us for our pains. Rousseau said that men are born free; and this saying, in its proper bearings, was and is a great and true saying; yet let it not lead us into the error of supposing that all men long for freedom and embrace it when it is offered to them. On the contrary, it has to be forced on them; and even then they will give it the slip if it is not religiously inculcated and strongly safeguarded.

Besides, men are born docile, and must in the nature of things remain so with regard to everything they do not understand. Now political science and the art of govemment are among the things they do not understand, and indeed are not at present allowed to understand. They can be enslaved by a system, as we are at present, because it happens to be there, and nobody understands it. An intelligently worked Capitalist system, as Comte saw, would give us all that most of us are intelligent enough to want. What makes it produce such unspeakably vile results is that it is an automatic system which is as little understood by those who profit by it in money as by those who are starved and degraded by it: our millionaires and statesmen are manifestly no more "captains of industry" or scientific politicians than our bookmakers are mathematicians. For some time past a significant word has been coming into use as a substitute for Destiny, Fate, and Providence. It is "The Machine": the machine that has no god in it. Why do governments do nothing in spite of reports of Royal Commissions that establish the most frightful urgency? Why do our philanthropic millionaires do nothing, though they are ready to throw bucketfuls of gold into the streets? The Machine will not let them. Always the Machine. In short, they dont know how.

They try to reform Society as an old lady might try to restore a broken down locomotive by prodding it with a knitting needle. And this is not at all because they are born fools, but because they have been educated, not into manhood and freedom, but into blindness and slavery by their parents and schoolmasters, themselves the victims of a similar misdirection, and consequently of The Machine. They do not want liberty. They have not been educated to want it. They choose slavery and inequality; and all the other evils are automatically added to them.

And yet we must have The Machine. It is only in unskilled hands under ignorant direction that machinery is dangerous. We can no more govern modern communities without political machinery than we can feed and clothe them without industrial machinery. Shatter The Machine, and you get Anarchy. And yet The Machine works so detestably at present that we have people who advocate Anarchy and call themselves Anarchists.

The Provocation to Anarchism

What is valid in Anarchism is that all Governments try to simplify their task by destroying liberty and glorifying authority in general and their own deeds in particular. But the difficulty in combining law and order with free institutions is not a natural one. It is a matter of inculcation. If people are brought up to be slaves, it is useless and dangerous to let them loose at the age of twenty-one and say "Now you are free." No one with the tamed soul and broken spirit of a slave can be free. It is like saying to a laborer brought up on a family income of thirteen shillings a week, "Here is one hundred thousand pounds: now you are wealthy." Nothing can make such a man really wealthy. Freedom and wealth are difficult and responsible conditions to which men must be accustomed and socially trained from birth. A nation that is free at twenty-one is not free at all; just as a man first enriched at fifty remains poor all his life, even if he does not curtail it by drinking himself to death in the first wild ecstasy of being able to swallow as much as he likes for the first time. You cannot govern men brought up as slaves otherwise than as slaves are governed. You may pile Bills of Right and Habeas Corpus Acts on Great Charters; promulgate American Constitutions; burn the chateaux and guillotine the seigneurs; chop off the heads of kings and queens and set up Democracy on the ruins of feudalism: the end of it all for us is that already in the twentieth century there has been as much brute coercion and savage intolerance, as much flogging and hanging, as much impudent injustice on the bench and lustful rancor in the pulpit, as much naive resort to torture, persecution, and suppression of free speech and freedom of the press, as much war, as much of the vilest excess of mutilation, rapine, and delirious indiscriminate slaughter of helpless non-combatants, old and young, as much prostitution of professional talent, literary and political, in defence of manifest wrong, as much cowardly sycophancy giving fine names to all this villainy or pretending that it is "greatly exaggerated," as we can find any record of from the days when the advocacy of liberty was a capital offence and Democracy was hardly thinkable. Democracy exhibits the vanity of Louis XIV, the savagery of Peter of Russia, the nepotism and provinciality of Napoleon, the fickleness of Catherine II: in short, all the childishnesses of all the despots without any of the qualities that enabled the greatest of them to fascinate and dominate their contemporaries.

And the flatterers of Democracy are as impudently servile to the successful, and insolent to common honest folk, as the flatterers of the monarchs. Democracy in America has led to the withdrawal of ordinary refined persons from politics; and the same result is coming in England as fast as we make Democracy as democratic as it is in America. This is true also of popular religion: it is so horribly irreligious that nobody with the smallest pretence to culture, or the least inkling of what the great prophets vainly tried to make the world understand, will have anything to do with it except for purely secular reasons.

Imagination

Before we can clearly understand how baleful is this condition of intimidation in which we live, it is necessary to clear up the confusion made by our use of the word imagination to denote two very different powers of mind. One is the power to imagine things as they are not: this I call the romantic imagination. The other is the power to imagine things as they are without actually sensing them; and this I will call the realistic imagination. Take for example marriage and war. One man has a vision of perpetual bliss with a domestic angel at home, and of flashing sabres, thundering guns, victorious cavalry charges, and routed enemies in the field. That is romantic imagination; and the mischief it does is incalculable. It begins in silly and selfish expectations of the impossible, and ends in spiteful disappointment, sour grievance, cynicism, and misanthropic resistance to any attempt to better a hopeless world. The wise man knows that imagination is not only a means of pleasing himself and beguiling tedious hours with romances and fairy tales and fools' paradises (a quite defensible and delightful amusement when you know exactly what you are doing and where fancy ends and facts begin), but also a means of foreseeing and being prepared for realities as yet unexperienced, and of testing the possibility and desirability of serious Utopias. He does not expect his wife to be an angel; nor does he overlook the facts that war depends on the rousing of all the murderous blackguardism still latent in mankind; that every victory means a defeat; that fatigue, hunger, terror, and disease are the raw material which romancers work up into military glory; and that soldiers for the most part go to war as children go to school, because they are afraid not to. They are afraid even to say they are afraid, as such candor is punishable by death in the military code.

A very little realistic imagination gives an ambitious person enormous power over the multitudinous victims of the romantic imagination. For the romancer not only pleases himself with fictitious glories: he also terrifies himself with imaginary dangers. He does not even picture what these dangers are: he conceives the unknown as always dangerous. When you say to a realist "You must do this" or "You must not do that," he instantly asks what will happen to him if he does (or does not, as the case may be). Failing an unromantic convincing answer, he does just as he pleases unless he can find for himself a real reason for refraining. In short, though you can intimidate him, you cannot bluff him. But you can always bluff the romantic person: indeed his grasp of real considerations is so feeble that you find it necessary to bluff him even when you have solid considerations to offer him instead. The campaigns of Napoleon, with their atmosphere of glory, illustrate this. In the Russian campaign Napoleon's marshals achieved miracles of bluff, especially Ney, who, with a handful of men, monstrously outnumbered, repeatedly kept the Russian troops paralyzed with terror by pure bounce. Napoleon himself, much more a realist than Ney (that was why he dominated him), would probably have surrendered; for sometimes the bravest of the brave will achieve successes never attempted by the cleverest of the clever. Wellington was a completer realist than Napoleon. It was impossible to persuade Wellington that he was beaten until he actually was beaten. He was unbluffable; and if Napoleon had understood the nature of Wellington's strength instead of returning Wellington's snobbish contempt for him by an academic contempt for Wellington, he would not have left the attack at Waterloo to Ney and D'Erlon, who, on that field, did not know when they were beaten, whereas Wellington knew precisely when he was not beaten. The unbluffable would have triumphed anyhow, probably, because Napoleon was an academic soldier, doing the academic thing (the attack in columns and so forth) with superlative ability and energy; whilst Wellington was an original soldier who, instead of outdoing the terrible academic columns with still more terrible and academic columns, outwitted them with the thin red line, not of heroes, but, as this uncompromising realist never hesitated to testify, of the scum of the earth.

Government by Bullies

These picturesque martial incidents are being reproduced every day in our ordinary life. We are bluffed by hardy simpletons and headstrong bounders as the Russians were bluffed by Ney; and our Wellingtons are threadbound by slave-democracy as Gulliver was threadbound by the Lilliputians. We are a mass of people living in a submissive routine to which we have been drilled from our childhood. When you ask us to take the simplest step outside that routine, we say shyly, "Oh, I really couldnt," or "Oh, I shouldnt like to," without being able to point out the smallest harm that could possibly ensue: victims, not of a rational fear of real dangers, but of pure abstract fear, the quintessence of cowardice, the very negation of "the fear of God." Dotted about among us are a few spirits relatively free from this inculcated paralysis, sometimes because they are half-witted, sometimes because they are unscrupulously selfish, sometimes because they are realists as to money and unimaginative as to other things, sometimes even because they are exceptionally able, but always because they are not afraid of shadows nor oppressed with nightmares. And we see these few rising as if by magic into power and affluence, and forming, with the millionaires who have accidentally gained huge riches by the occasional windfalls of our commerce, the governing class. Now nothing is more disastrous than a governing class that does not know how to govern. And how can this rabble of the casual products of luck, cunning, and folly, be expected to know how to govern? The merely lucky ones and the hereditary ones do not owe their position to their qualifications at all. As to the rest, the realism which seems their essential qualification often consists not only in a lack of romantic imagination, which lack is a merit, but of the realistic, constructive, Utopian imagination, which lack is a ghastly defect. Freedom from imaginative illusion is therefore no guarantee whatever of nobility of character: that is why inculcated submissiveness makes us slaves to people much worse than ourselves, and why it is so important that submissiveness should no longer be inculcated.

And yet as long as you have the compulsory school as we know it, we shall have submissiveness inculcated. What is more, until the active hours of child life are organized separately from the active hours of adult life, so that adults can enjoy the society of children in reason without being tormented, disturbed, harried, burdened, and hindered in their work by them as they would be now if there were no compulsory schools and no children hypnotized into the belief that they must tamely go to them and be imprisoned and beaten and over-tasked in them, we shall have schools under one pretext or another; and we shall have all the evil consequences and all the social hopelessness that result from turning a nation of potential freemen and freewomen into a nation of two-legged spoilt spaniels with everything crushed out of their nature except dread of the whip. Liberty is the breath of life to nations; and liberty is the one thing that parents, schoolmasters, and rulers spend their lives in extirpating for the sake of an immediately quiet and finally disastrous life.

This text was taken from a printed volume containing the plays "Misalliance", "The Dark Lady of the Sonnets", "Fanny's First Play", and the essay "A Treatise on Parents and Children".

www.ingramcontent.com/pod-product-compliance
Lightning Source LLC
LaVergne TN
LVHW090946080826
845145LV00003B/910

* 9 7 8 1 5 9 5 4 0 2 3 5 6 *